Doodle Fun Mid Size Coloring Book

By Artist Dwyanna Stoltzfus

Copyright © 2016 by Dwyanna Stoltzfus

ALL RIGHTS RESERVED

ISBN-10:1537516744

ISBN-13:978-1537516745

This publication is for personal use only.
No part of this publication may be reproduced, stored in a retrieval
System, or transmitted in any form or by any means – electronic, mechanical, photocopy,
Or any other - without the written permission
of the artist/publisher – Dwyanna Stoltzfus.

Unauthorized reproduction of any part of this publication by any means
Is an infringement of copyright.
All artwork and images in this publication are
Protected by copyright laws.

Join the Fun!!
Share your colored pages!!

You are invited to color the pages
From this and all publications by
Dwyanna Stoltzfus. Then scan and post
Your colored creations in
Coloring with Dwyanna
Adult Coloring Group
On facebook
https://web.facebook.com/groups/151935762835
6169/?_rdr
Join Coloring with Dwyanna Coloring Group,
And have fun sharing your colored pages
And meeting new coloring friends.
Members of the group will also have access
To free coloring pages.
You are welcome to share your colored pages on
Any social network, make sure to mention the title of
The book and the author/artist name.
Uncolored images may not be shared.

Check out my blog at:
coloringwithdwyanna.blogspot.com7

PDF Printable coloring pages available
On Etsy at
https://www.etsy.com/people/dwyannastoltzfus

Follow Dwyanna's art on facebook at
Oodles of Doodles Designs –
Adult Coloring Books by
Dwyanna Stoltzfus
https://web.facebook.com/Oodles-of-Doodles-Designs-Adult-Coloring-Books-by-Dwyanna-Stoltzfus-743502922387046/

Acknowledgments

Thank You to my family for all your support
of my art and this project.
I could not have done it without you!!

Thank You God for the gift and love
Of art and drawing!!

About:

Get ready to color 31 fun doodle art designs by Artist Dwyanna Stoltzfus. This coloring book will provide many hours of fun, entertainment. It will also provide hours of peaceful calm and relaxation.

Coloring is not just for children. We encourage our precious children to draw and color as a relaxing quiet activity. Coloring can have the same relaxing/calming effect on adults. It is especially beneficial to those who struggle with anxiety or stress. It's the perfect stress relief.

In this adult coloring book you will find 31 amazing illustrations, printed one per page. A collection of fun images inspired by doodle art. You will find beautiful intricate flowers, swirls, cats, a cupcake, A teddy bear, and more!!

You can use this coloring book to help you relax and unwind or just to have fun. You can color the illustrations simply or add depth by shading. Crayons is not recommended for the intricate detail but can be Used on some of the pages. You can also color with fine tip markers, gel pens, and colored pencils.

Enjoy the experience of coloring!!

But most of all relax and have fun!!

Coloring tips:

If you desire to add depth to your coloring you can shade with colored pencils. Use dark colors around edges and into the peaks. Blend in light colors for the middle and more open spaces. You can use black to darken areas, and white to lighten and brighten areas.

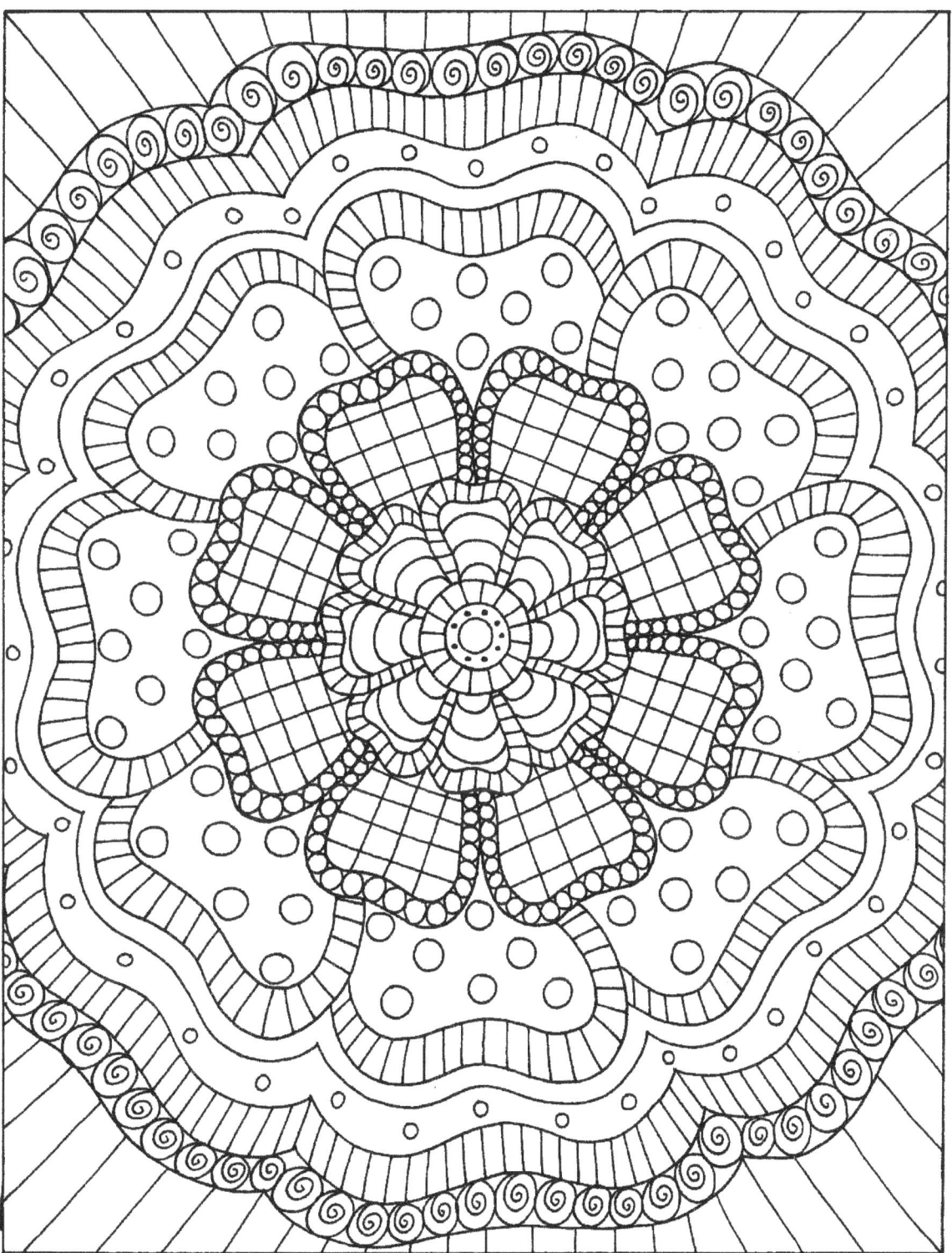

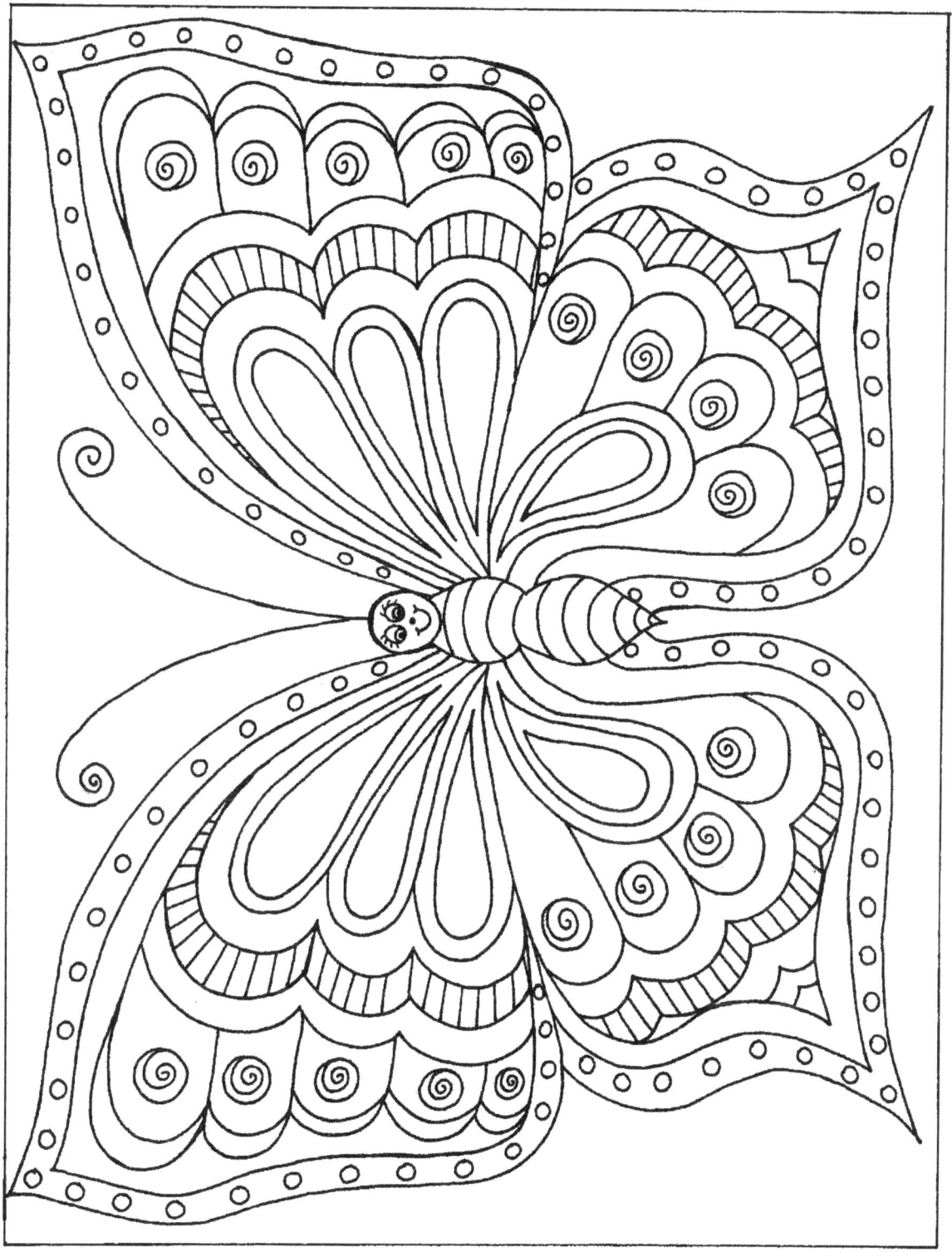

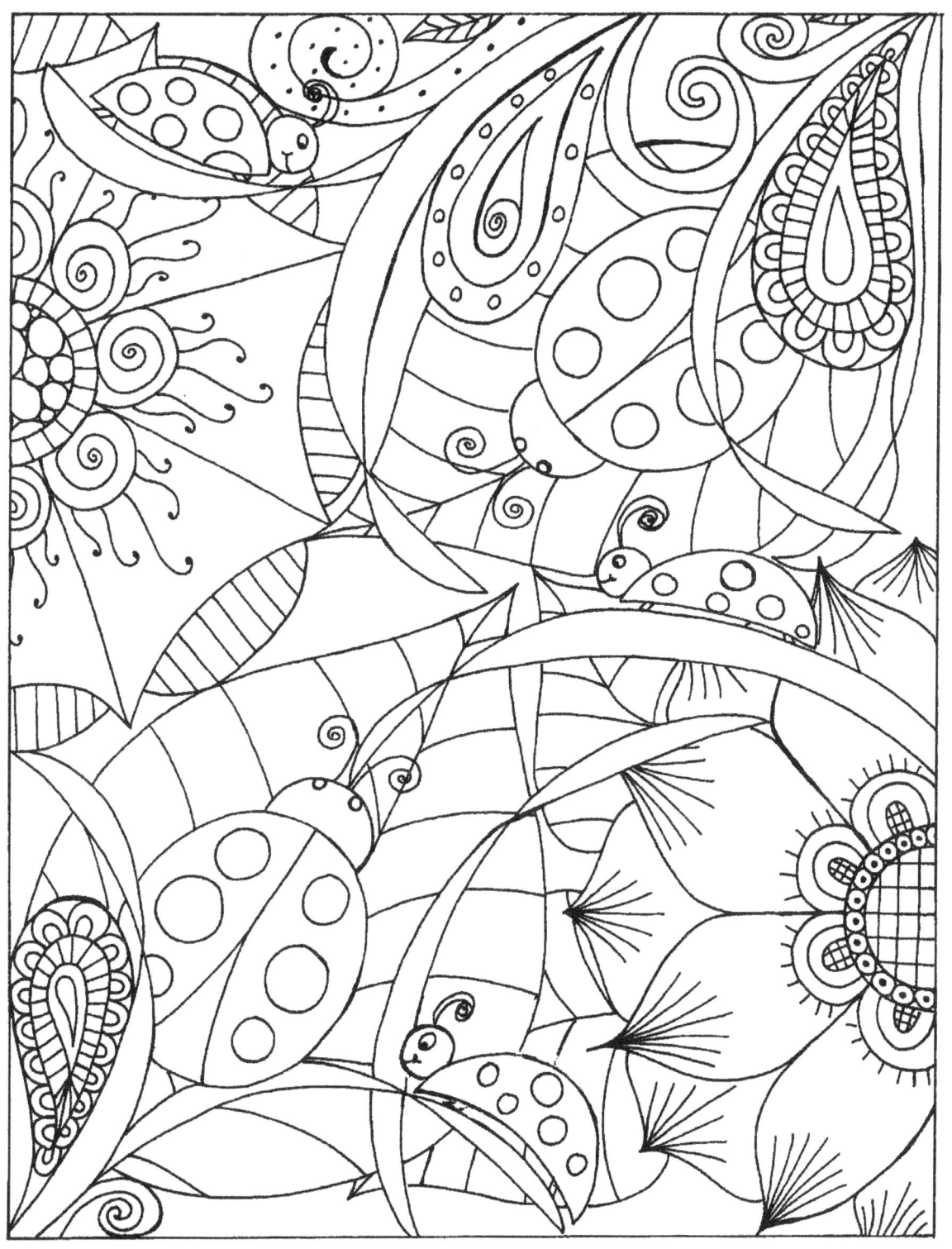

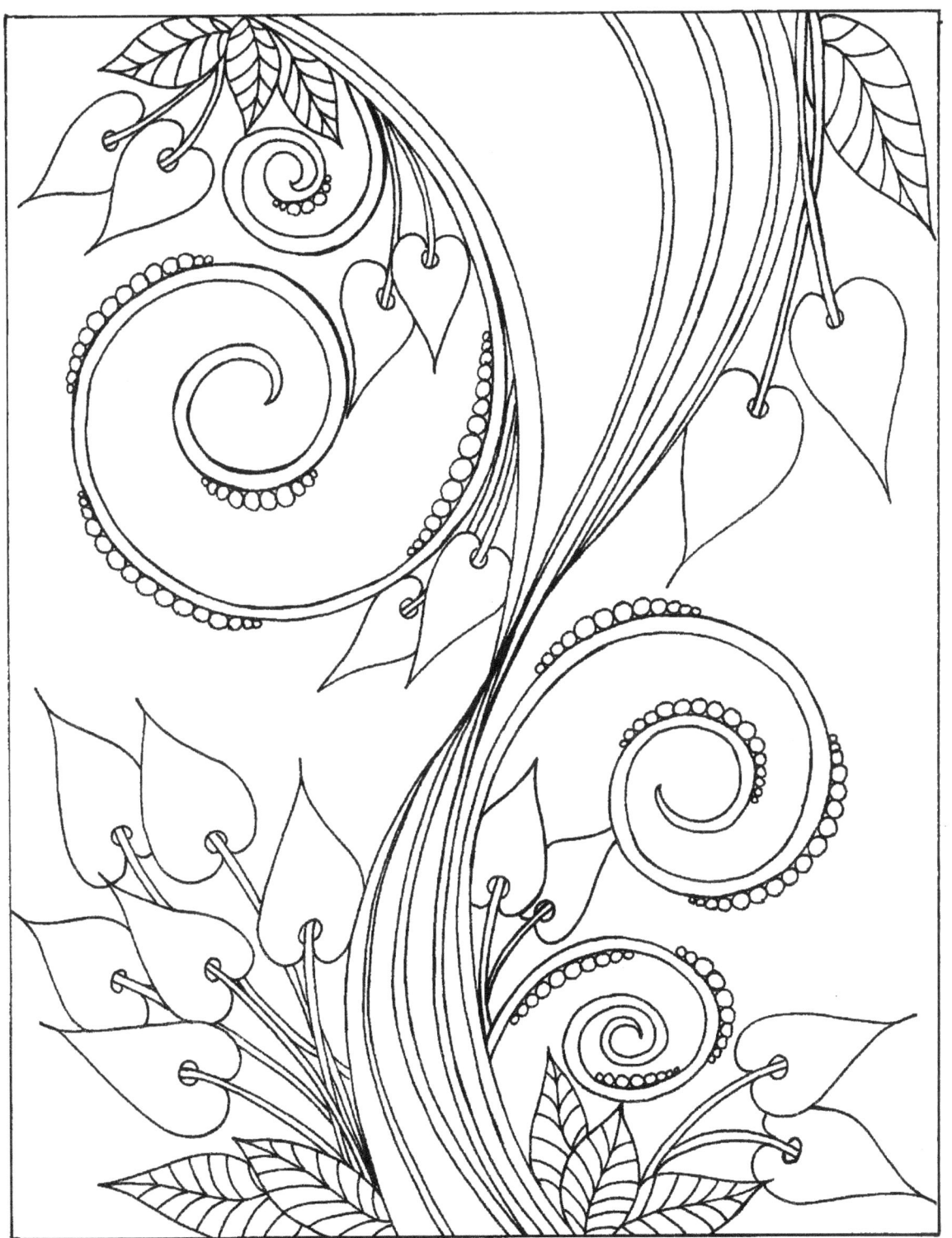

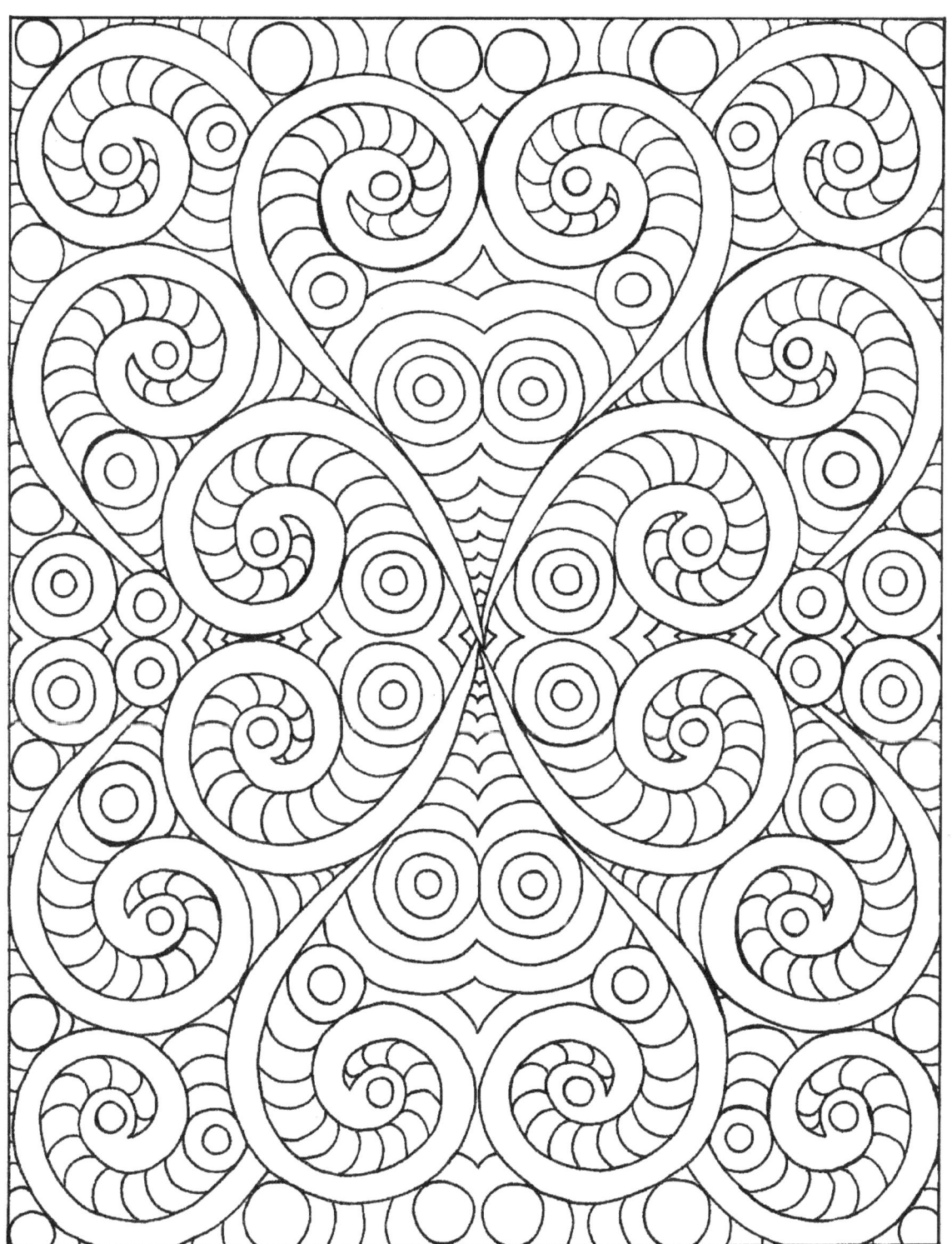

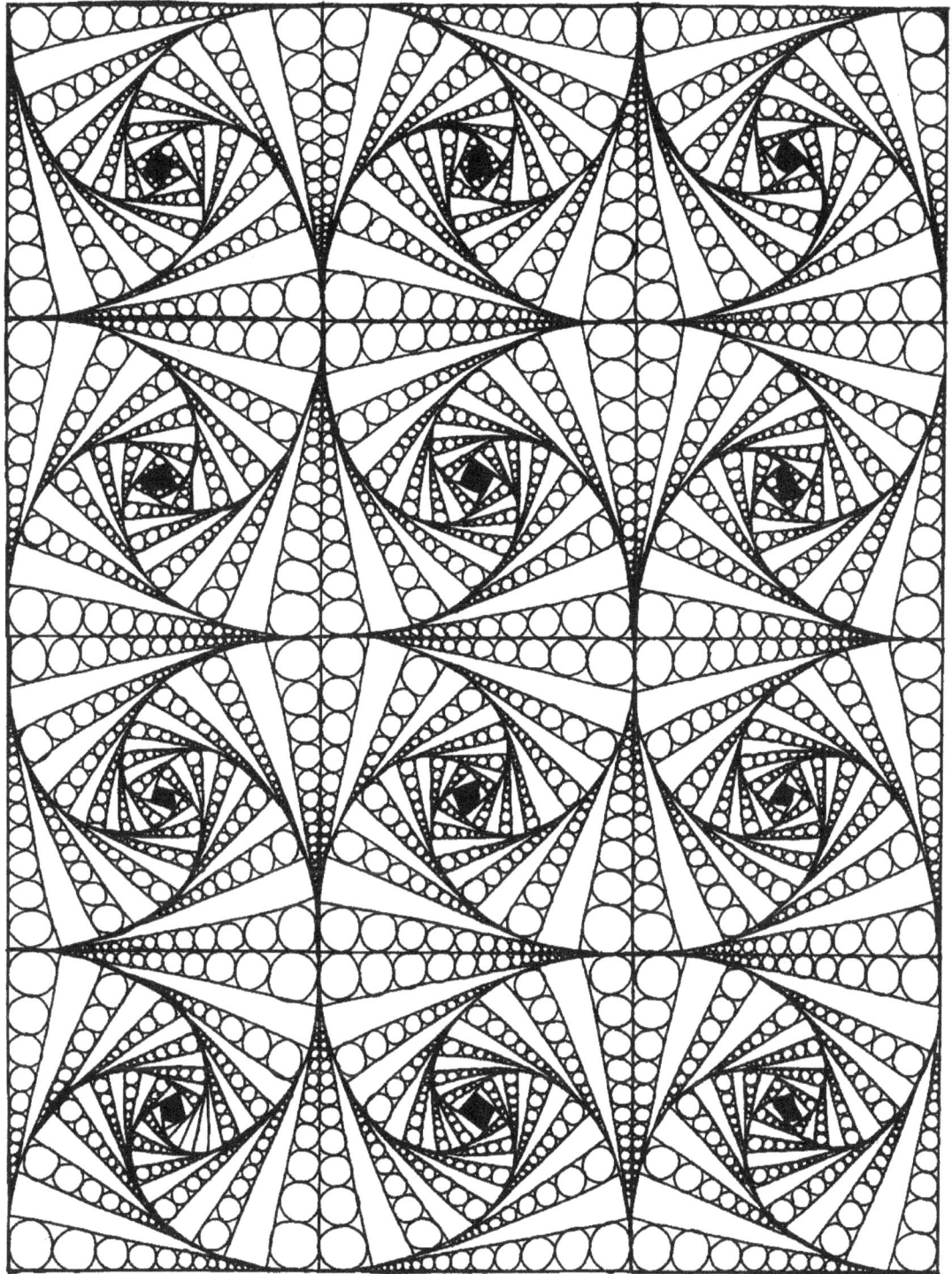

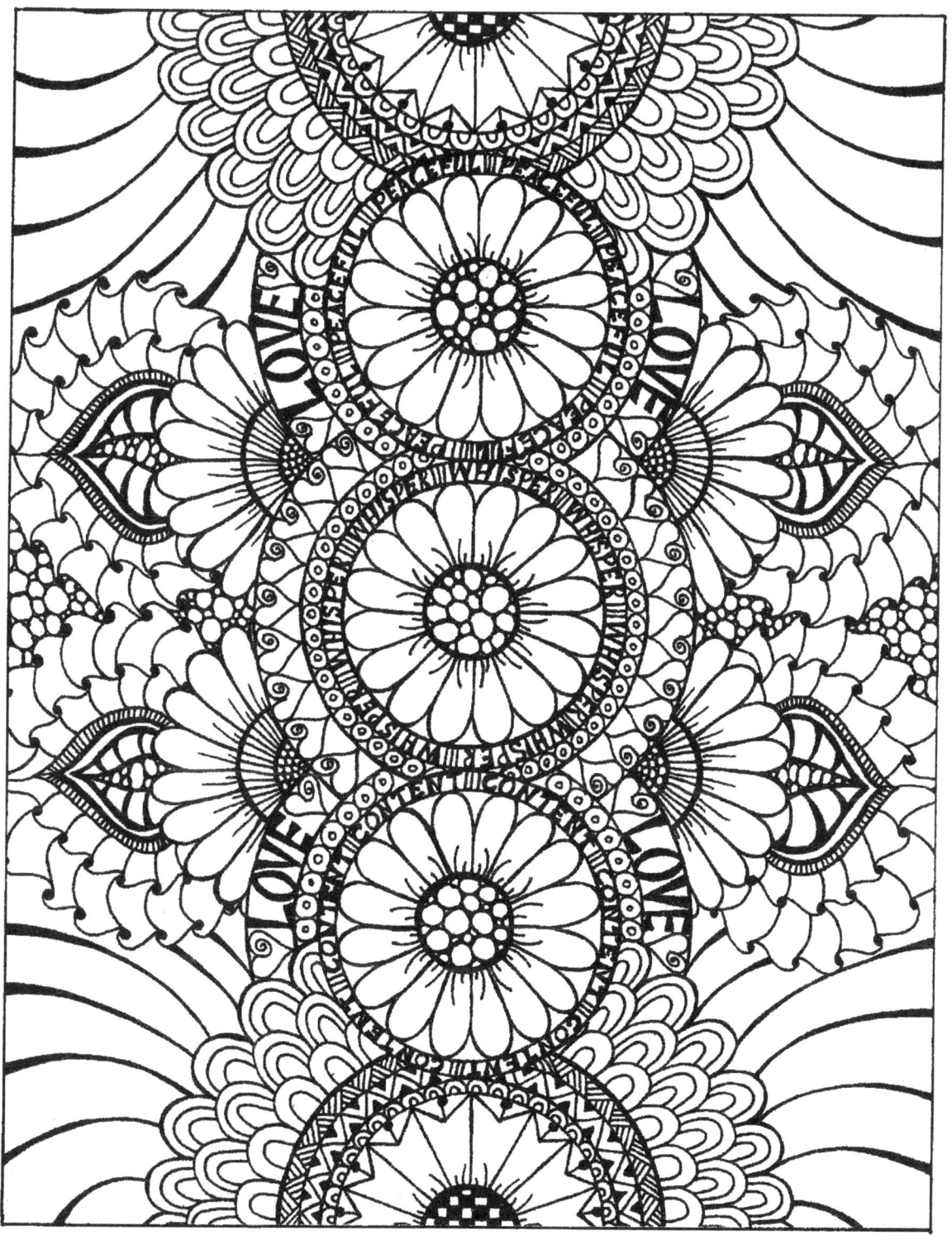

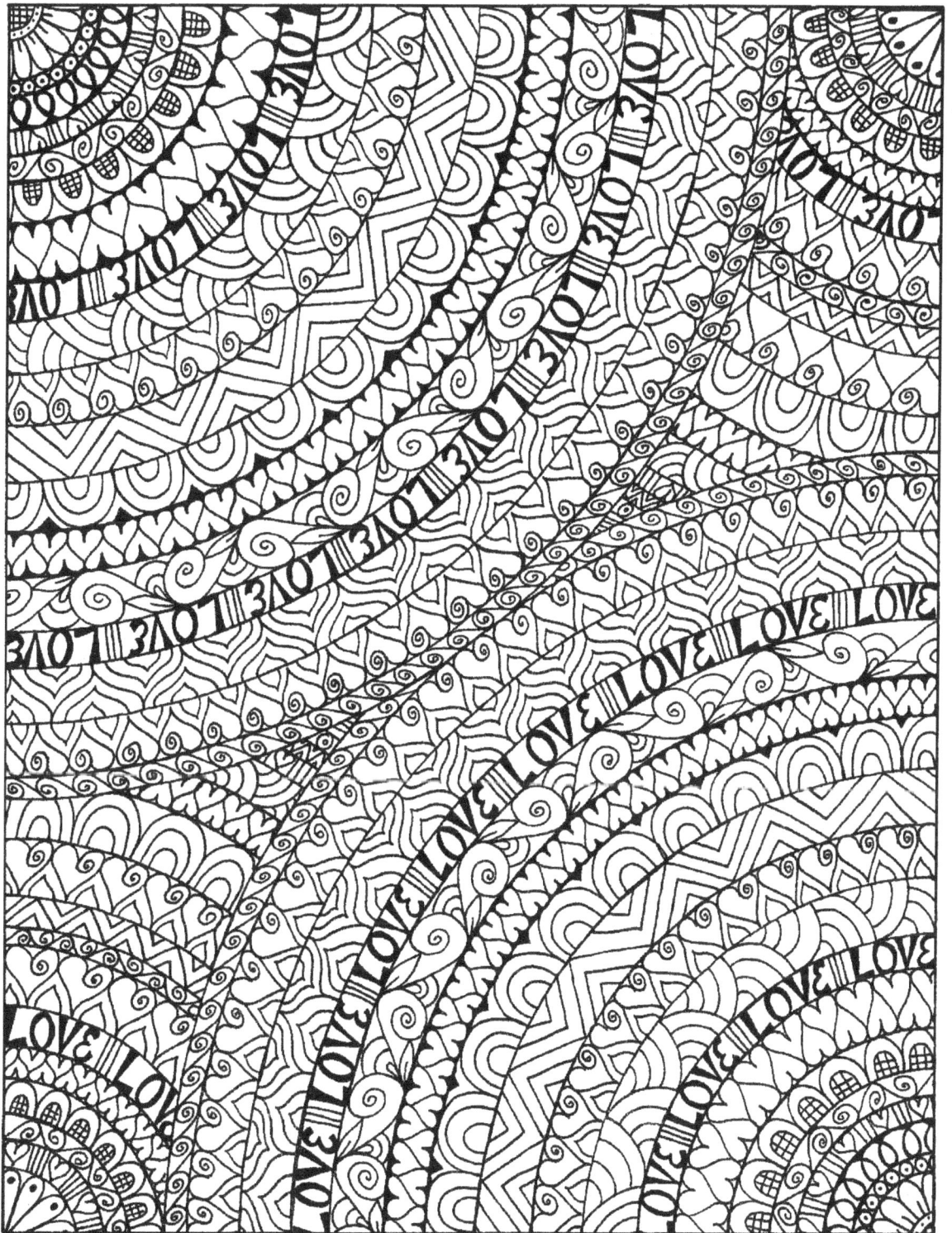

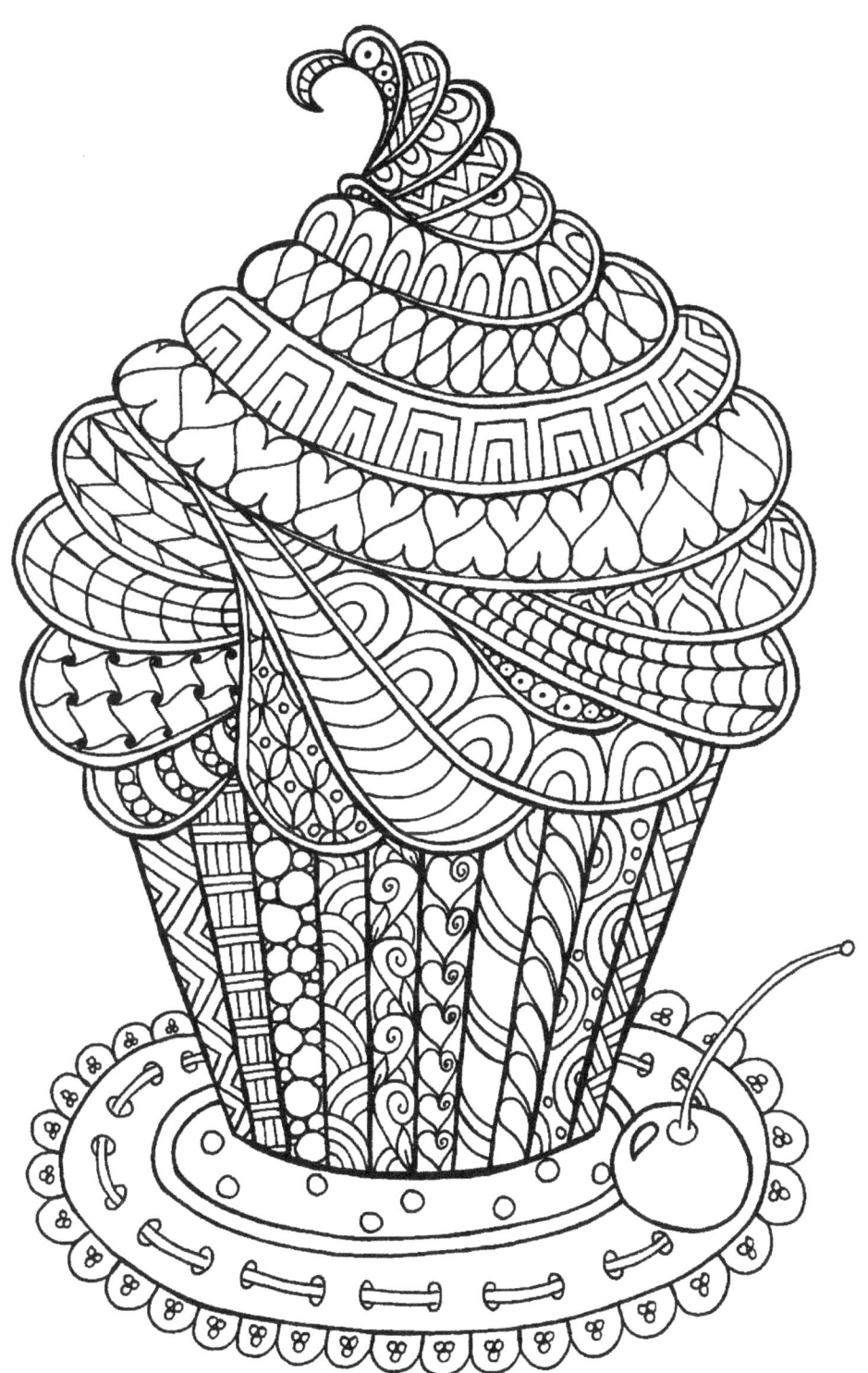

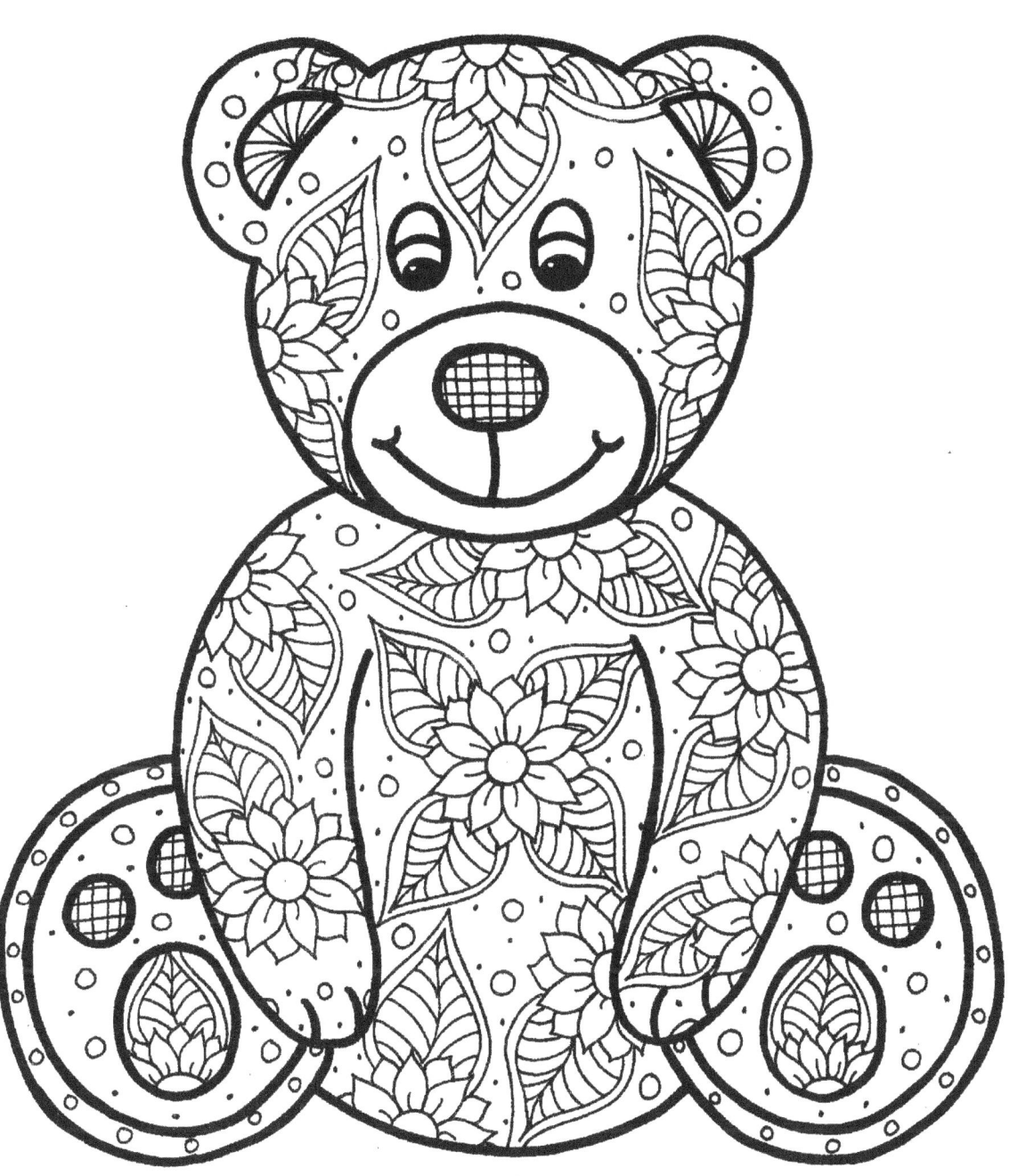

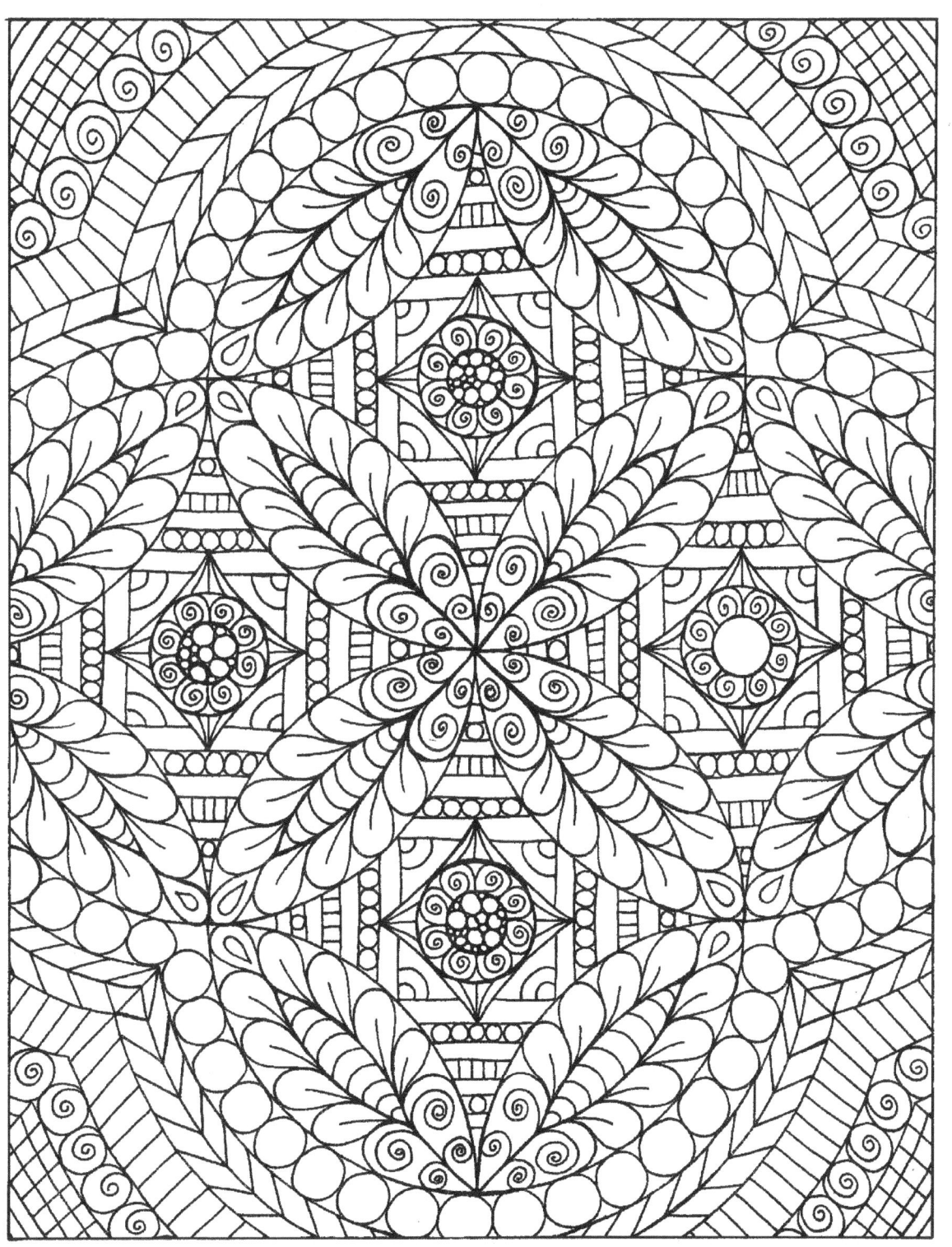

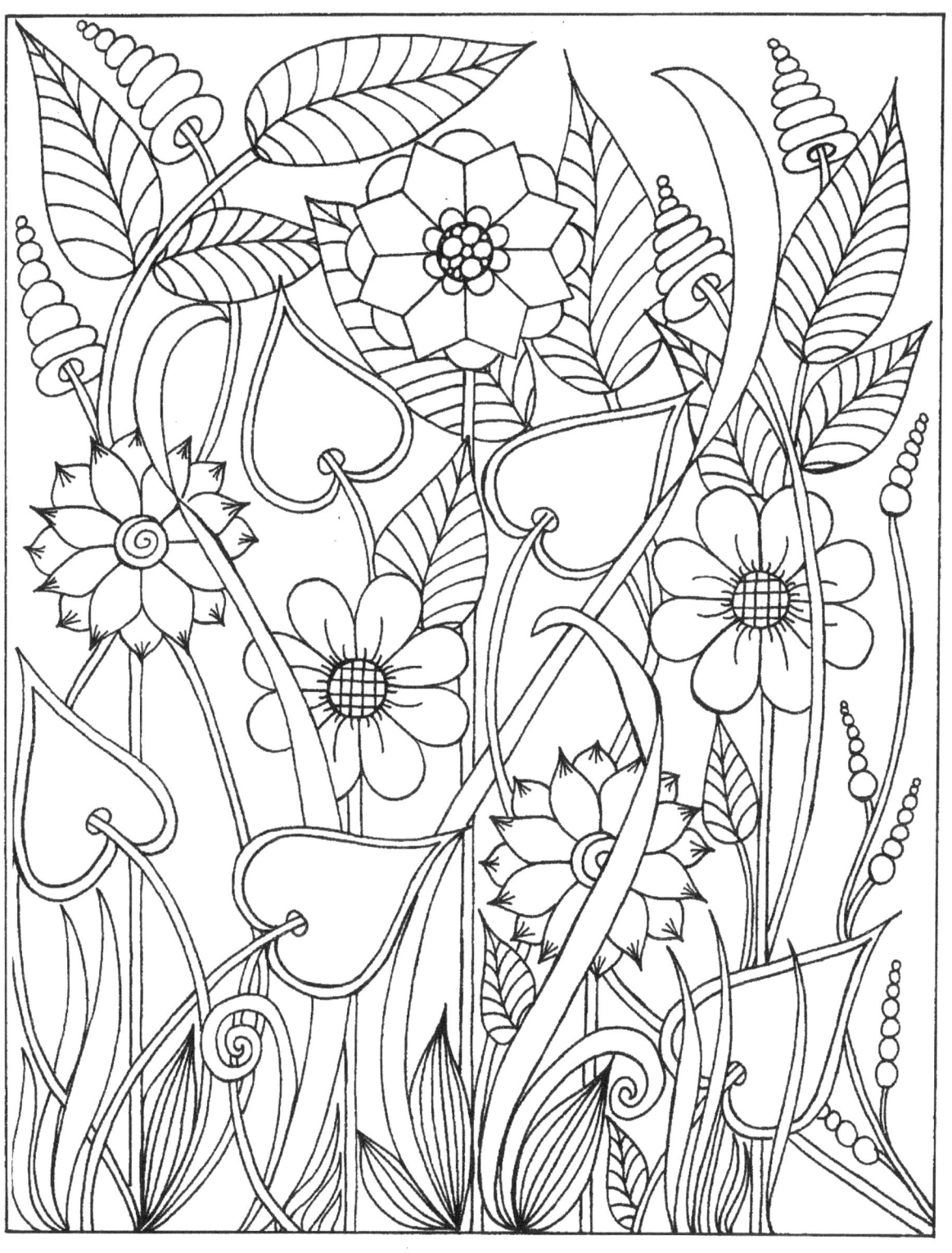

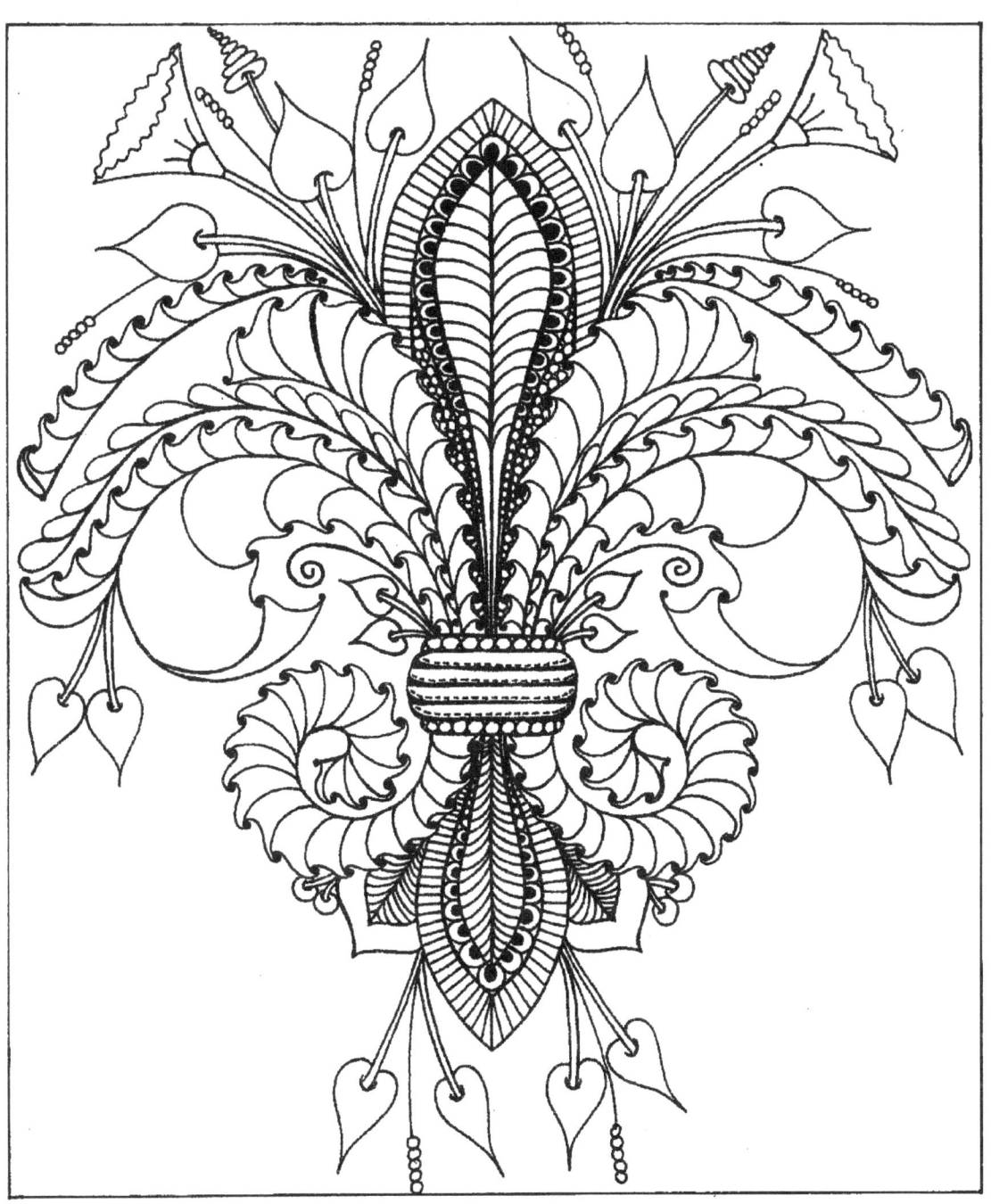

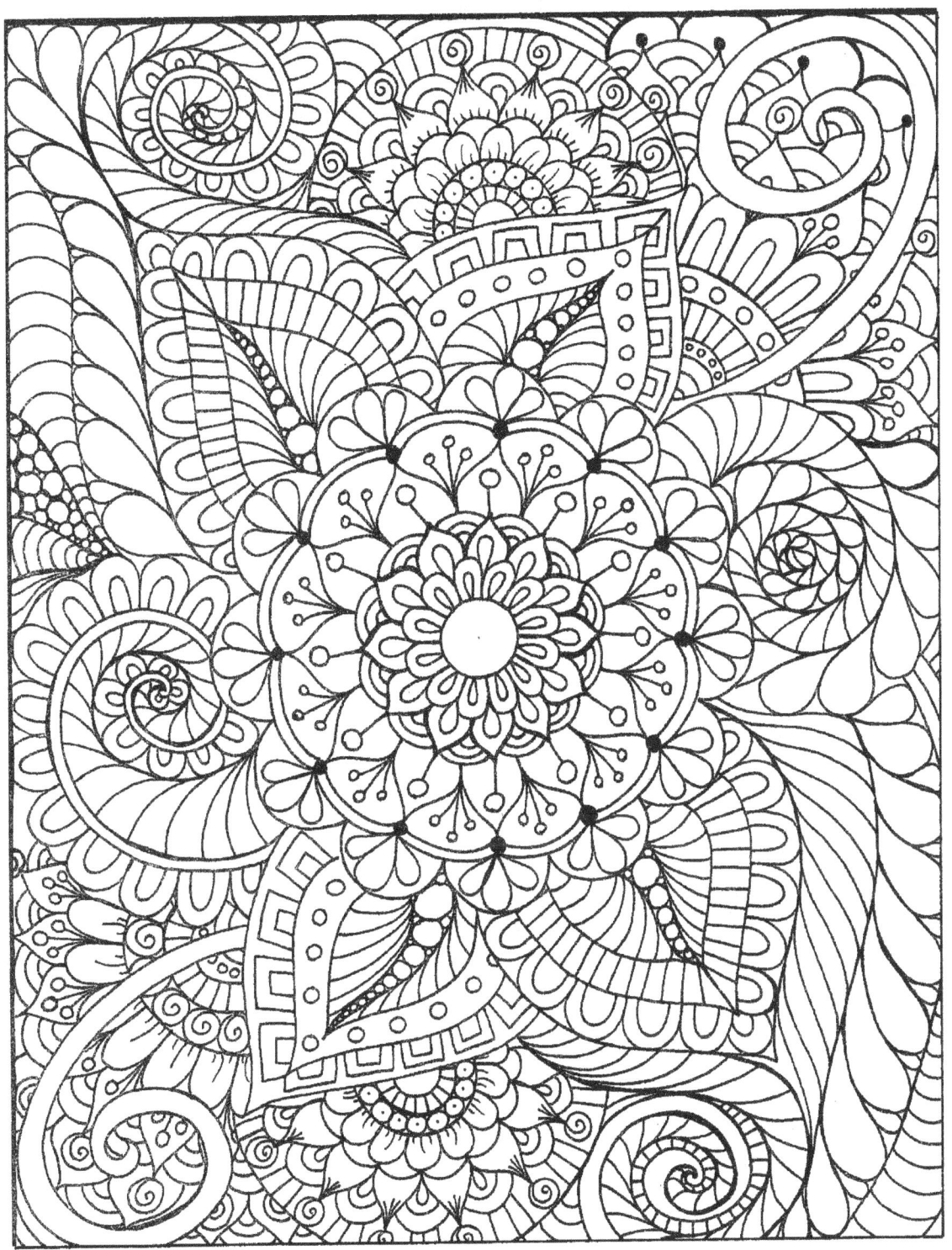

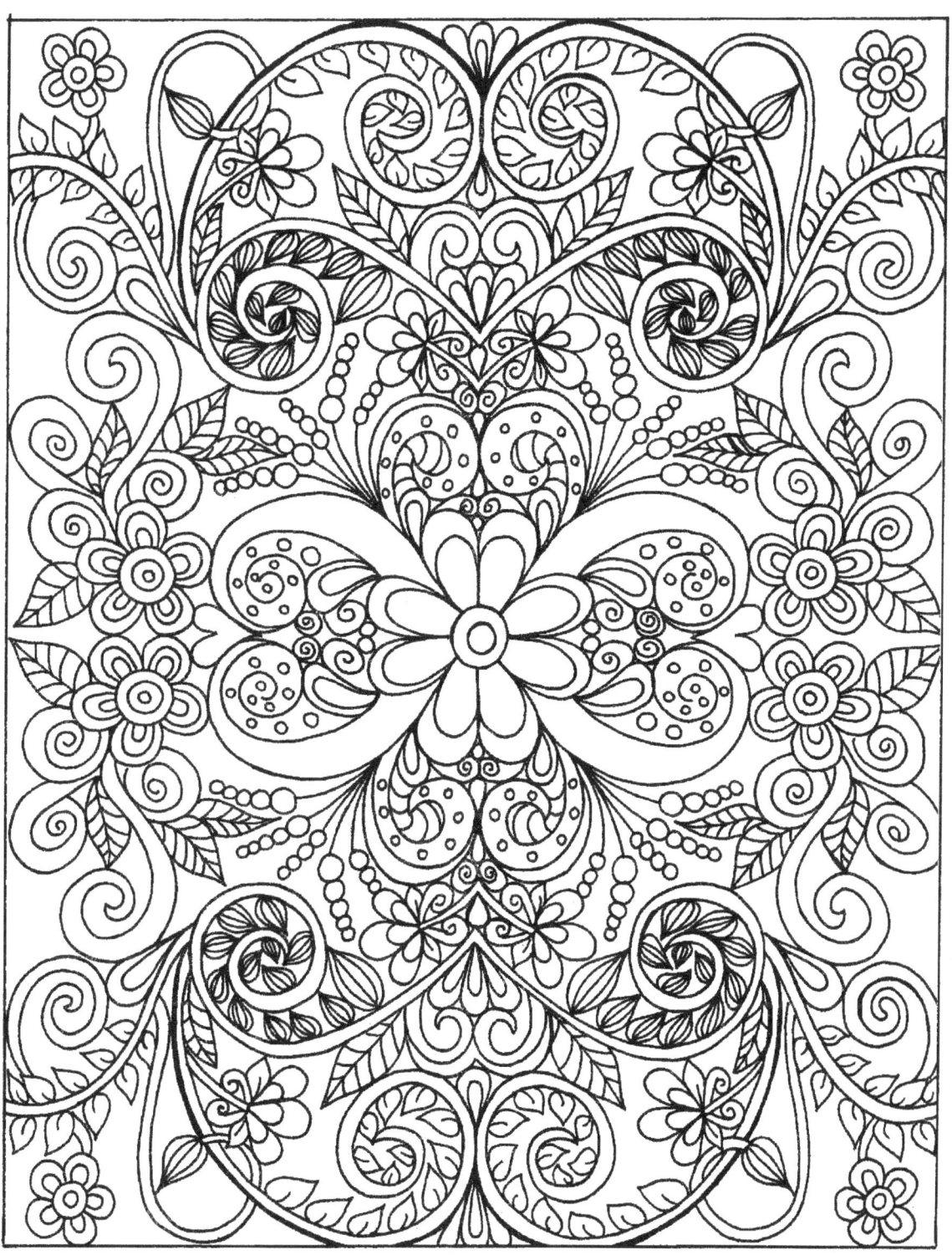

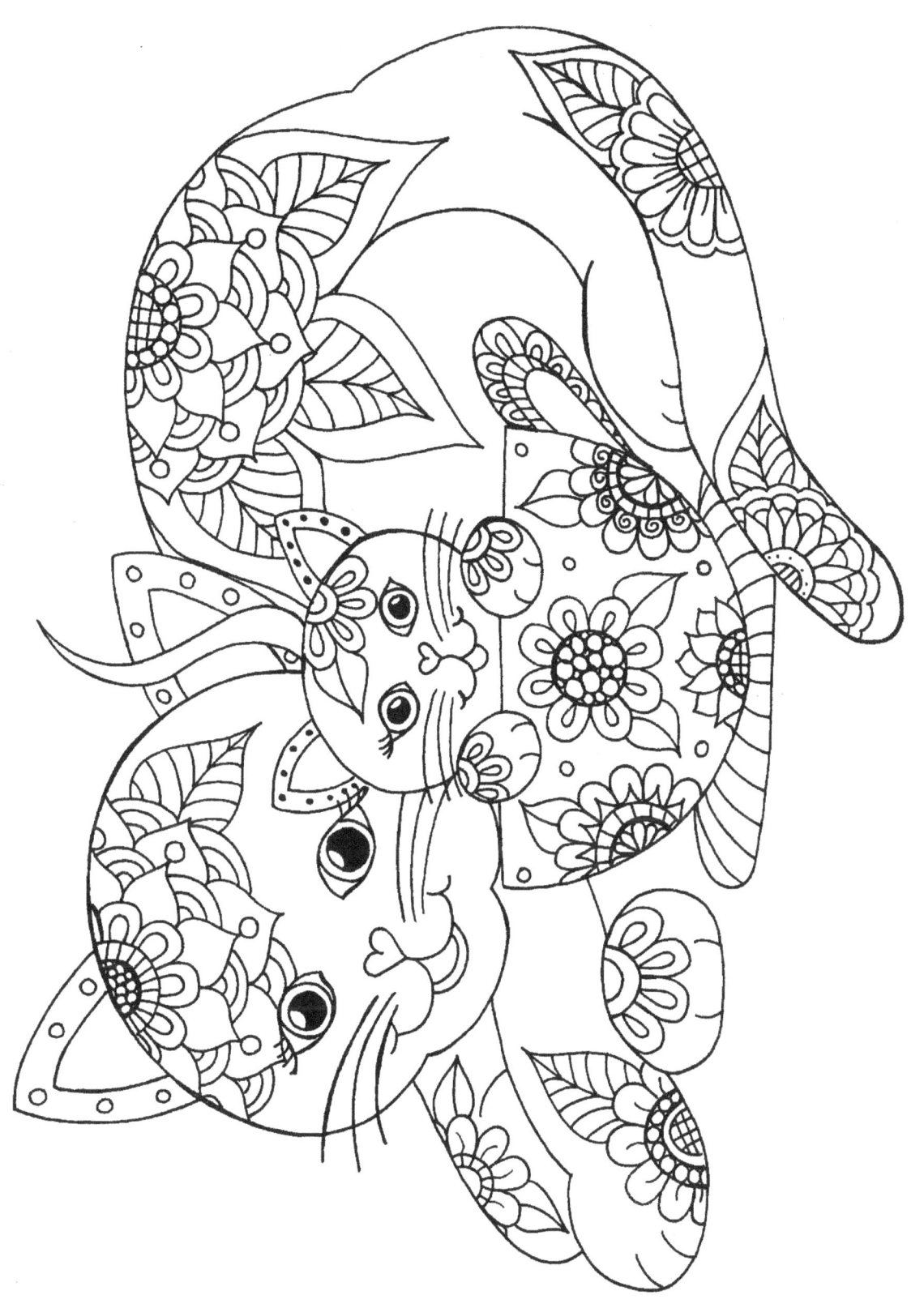

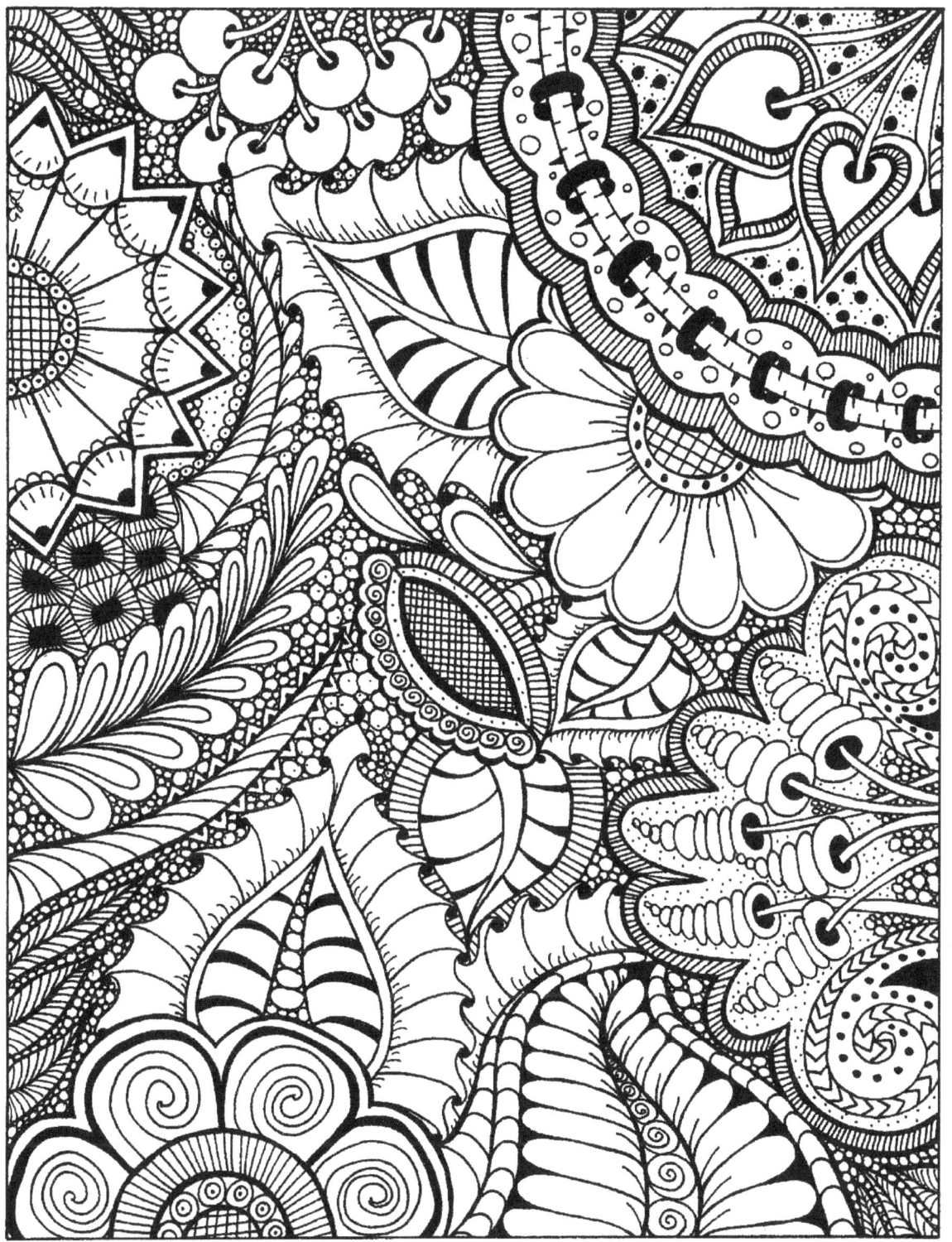

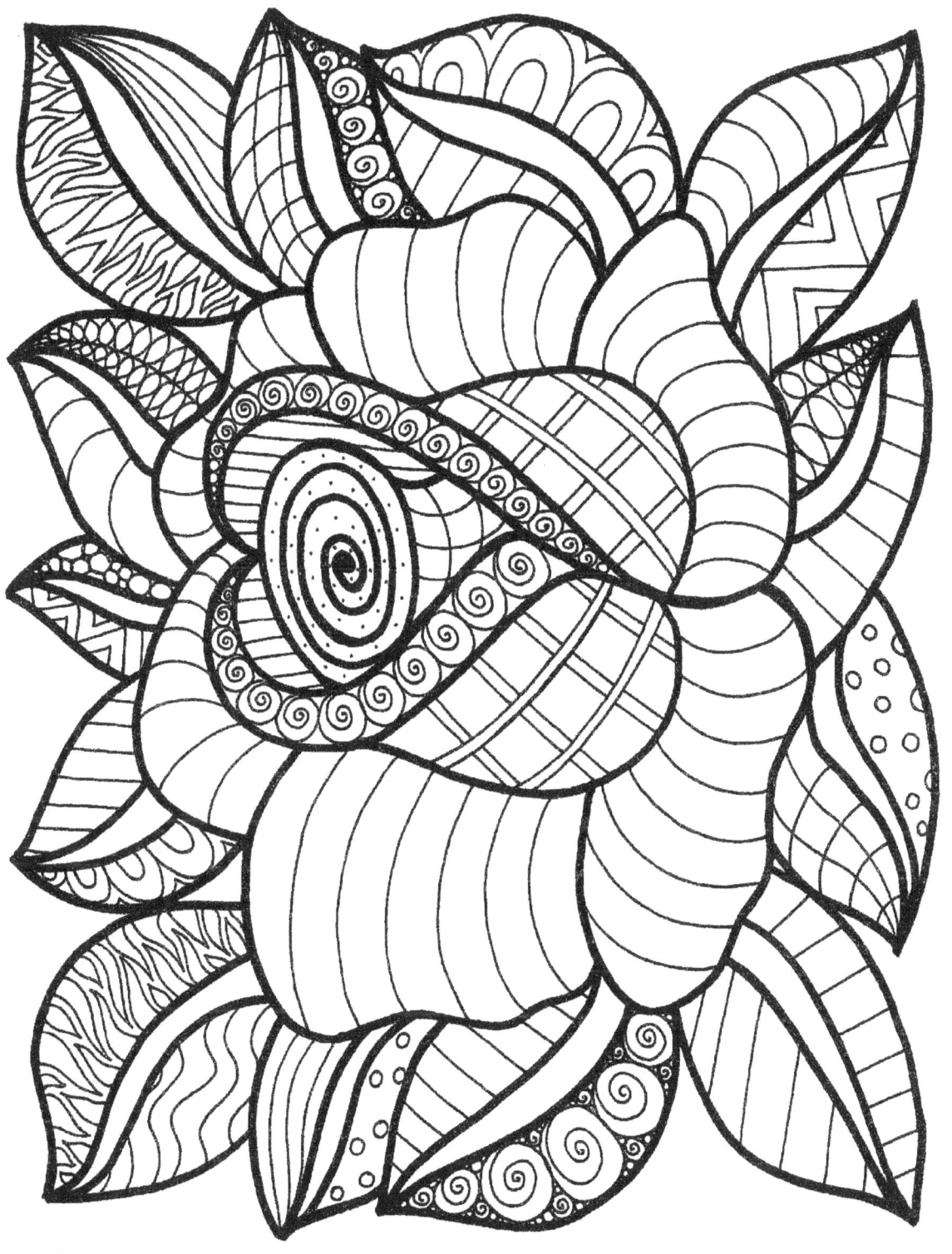

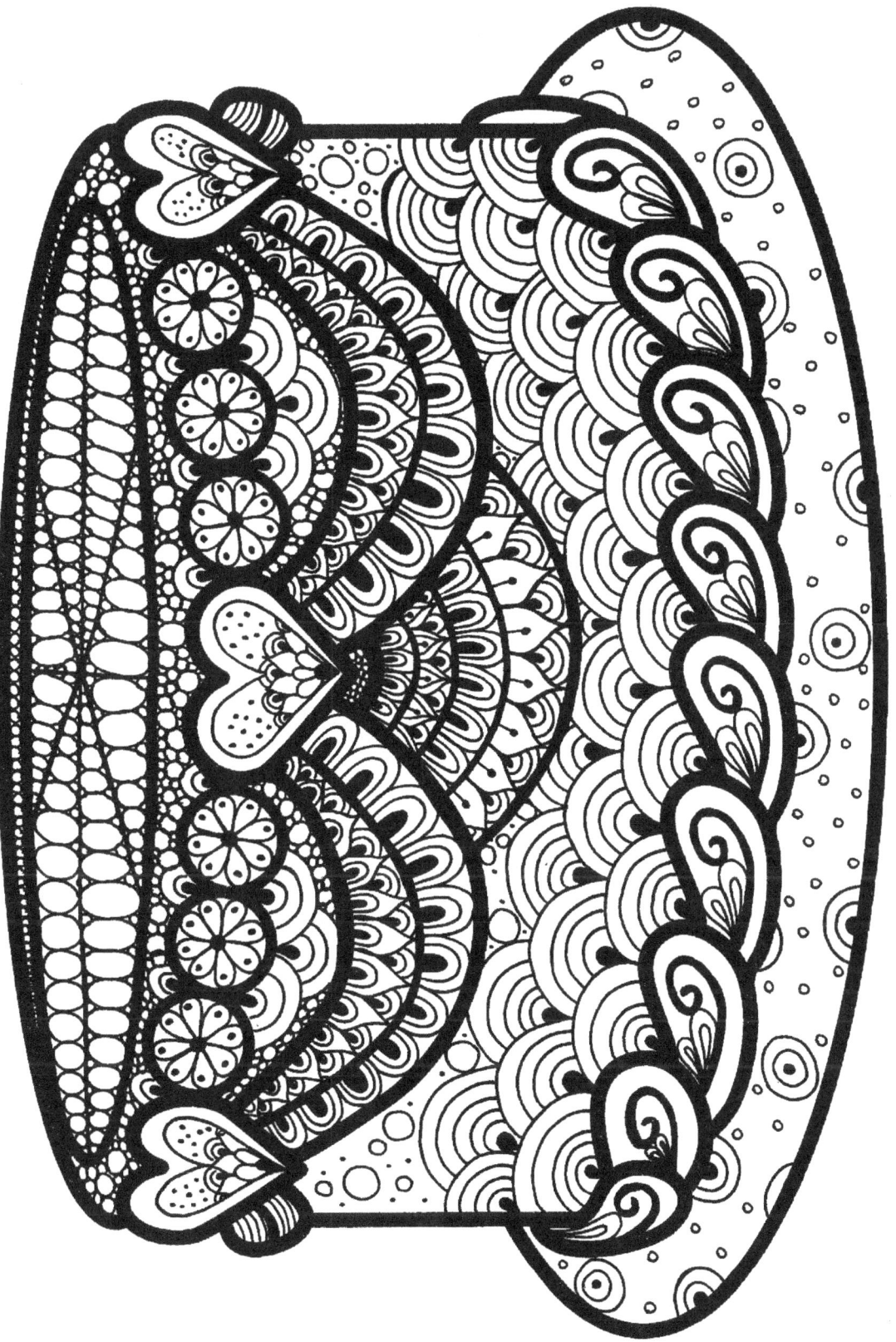

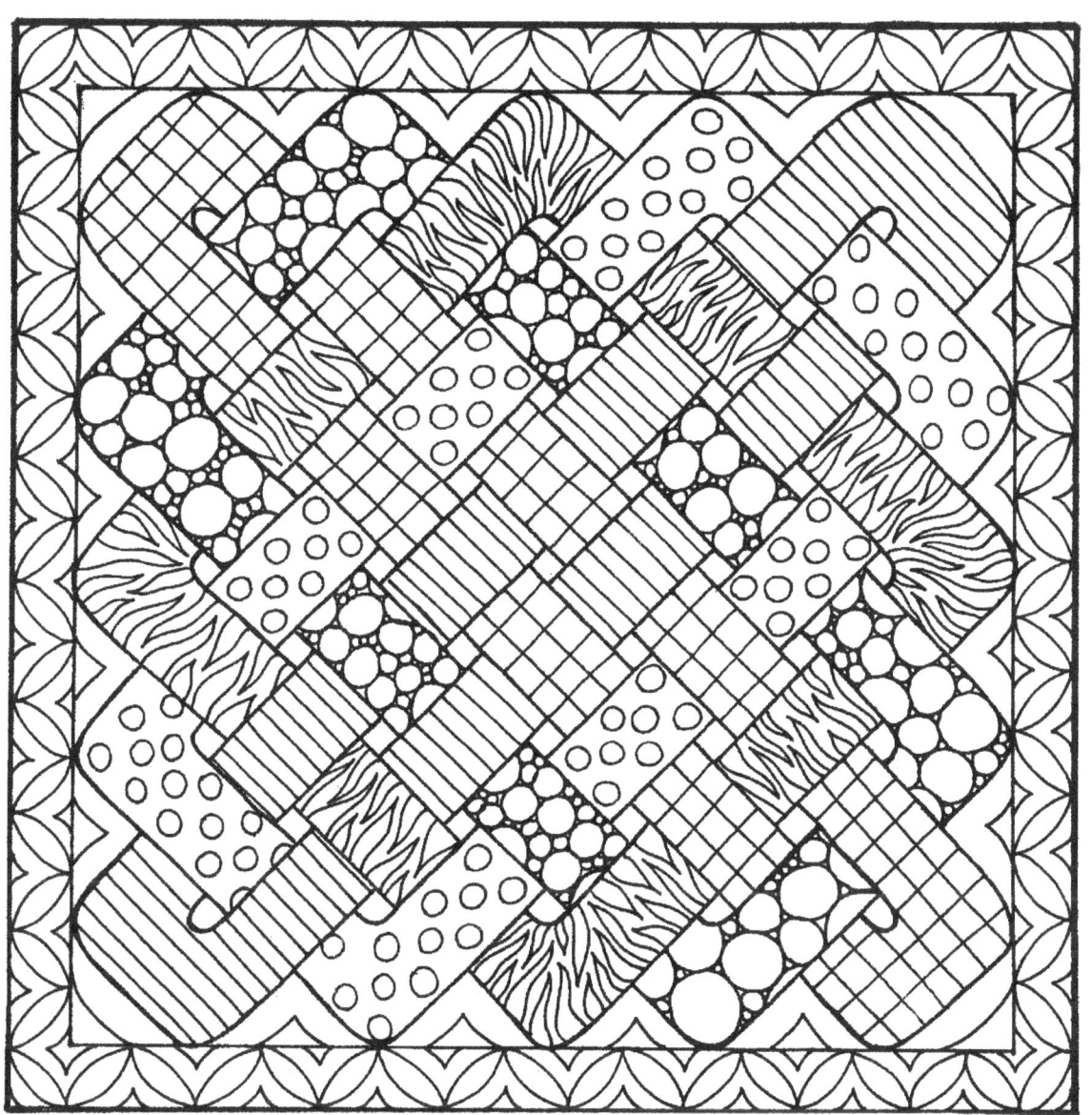

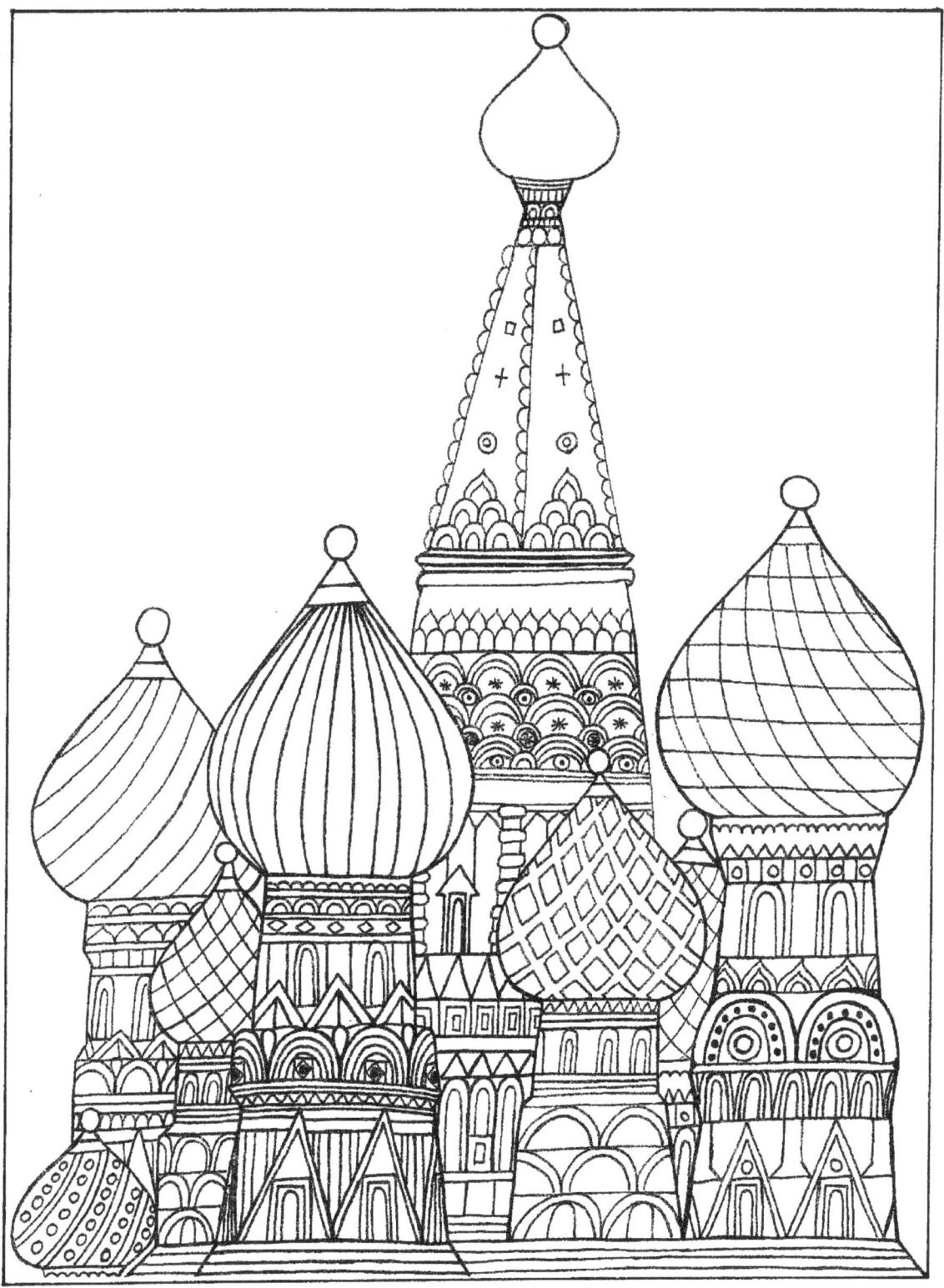

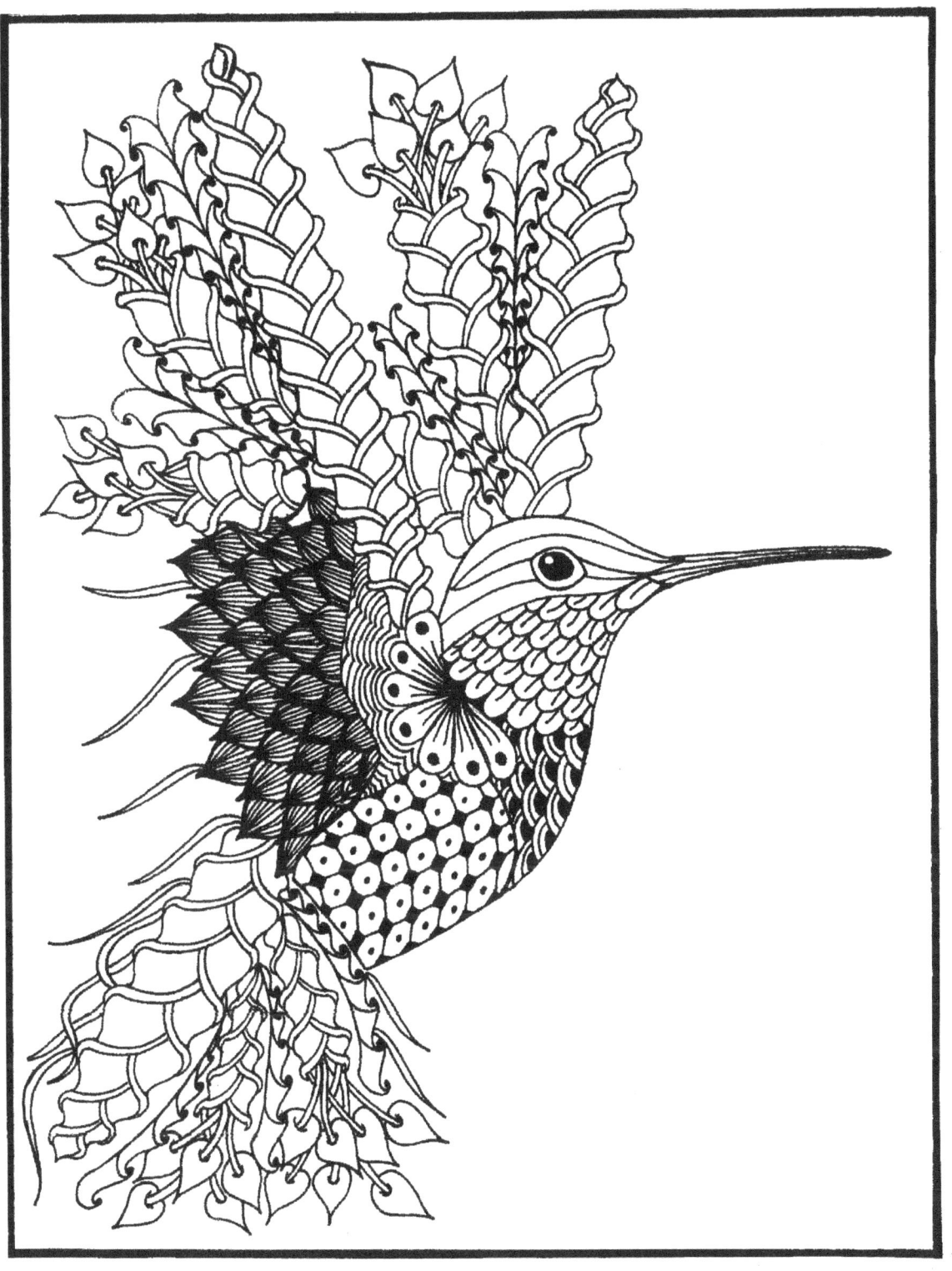

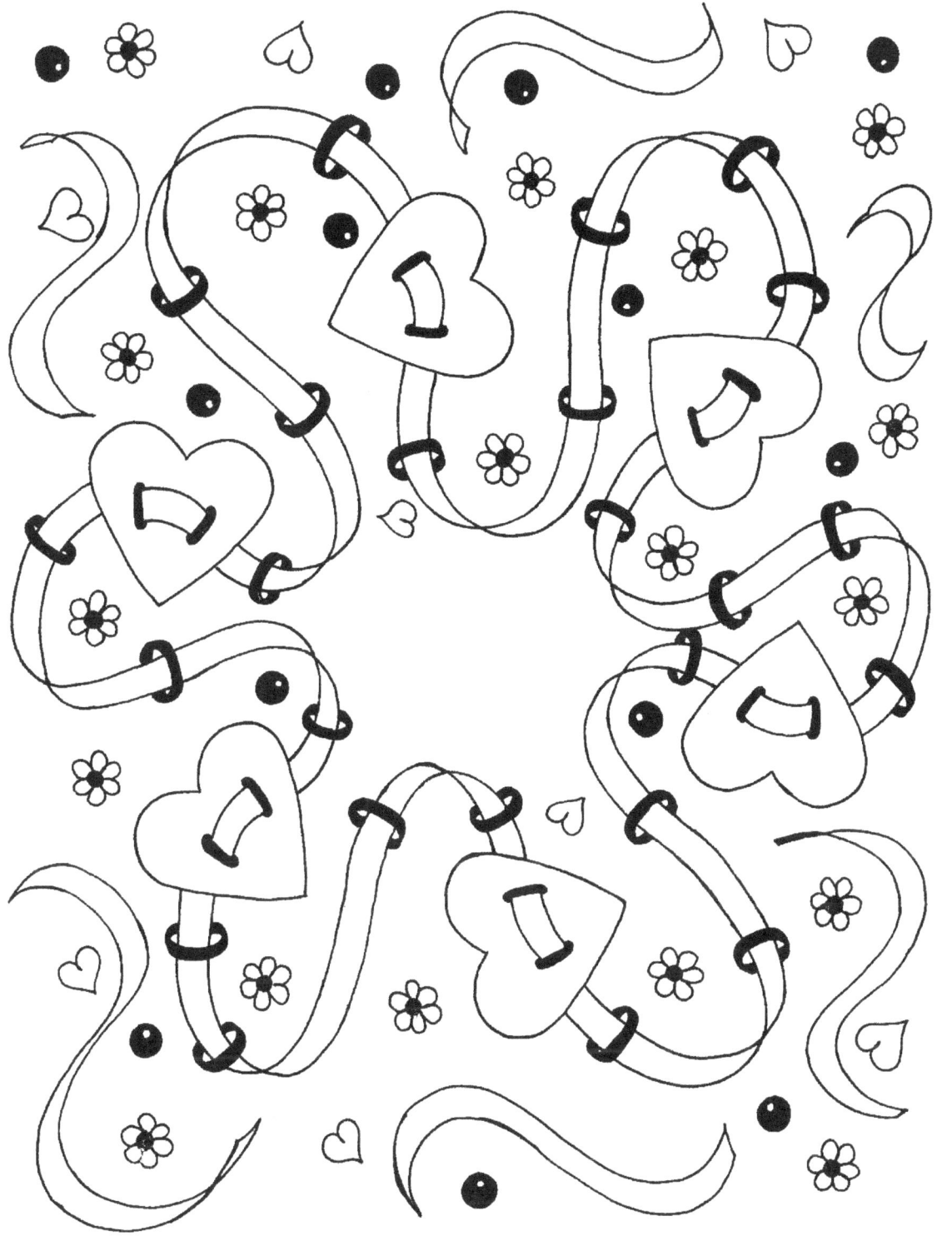

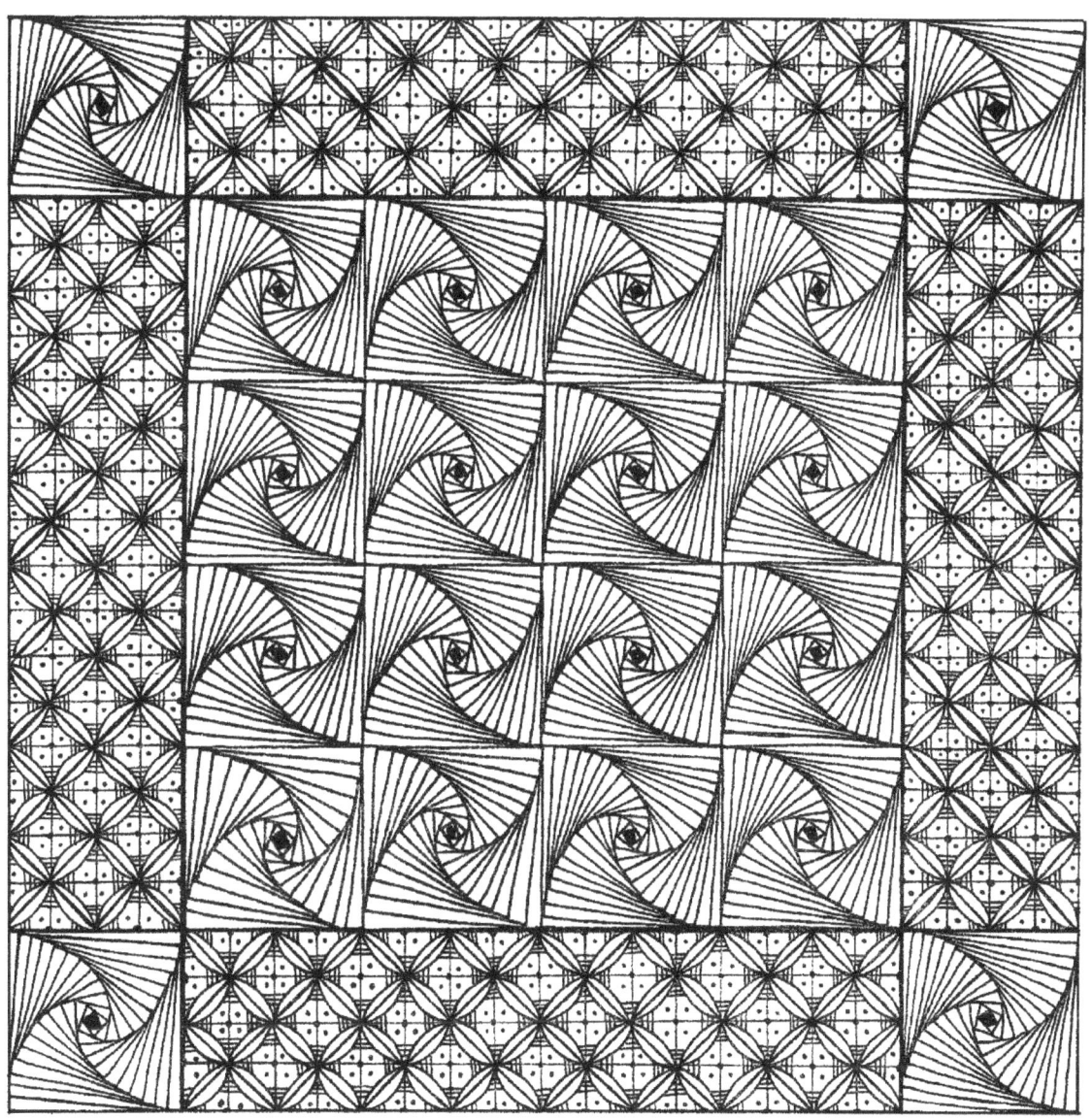

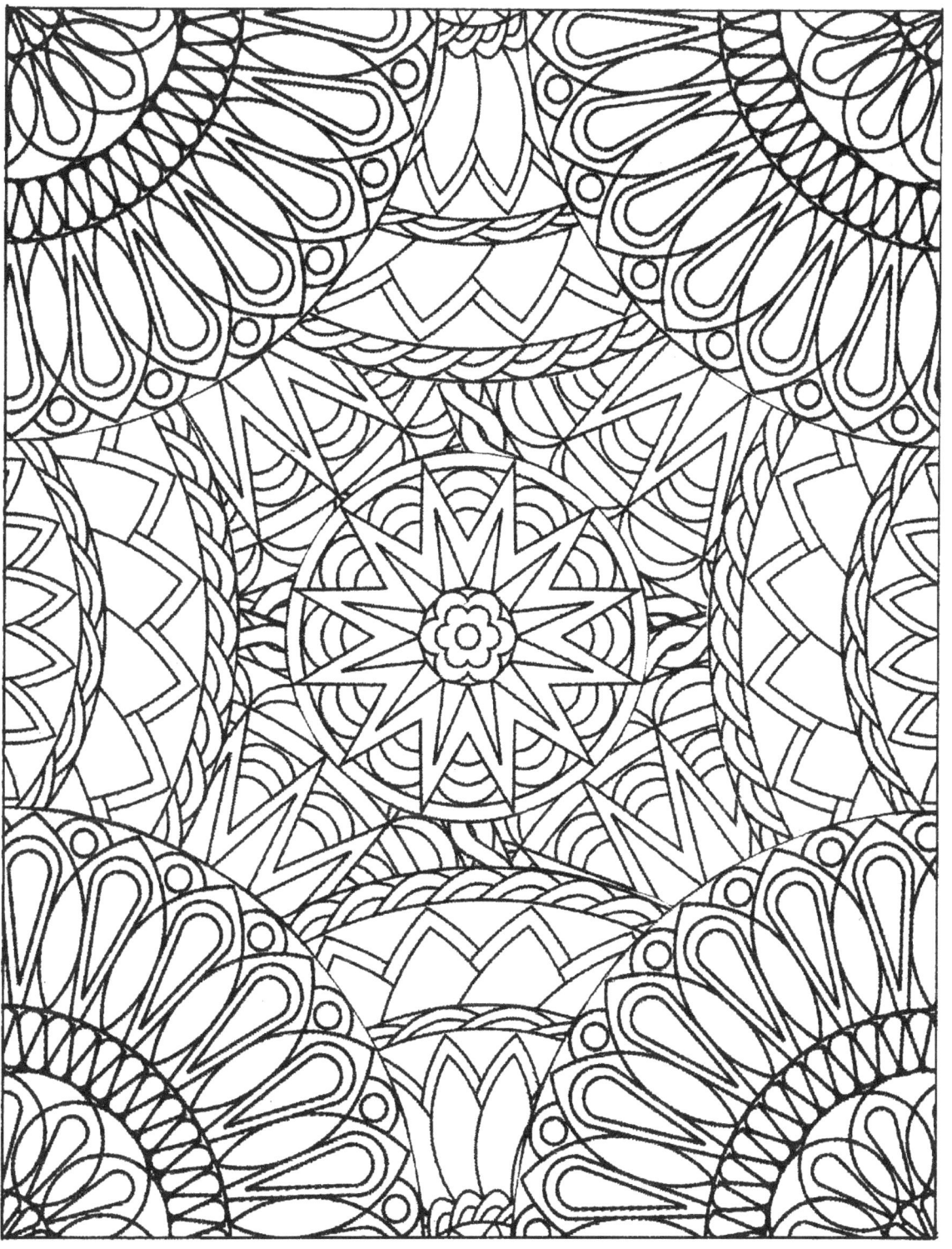

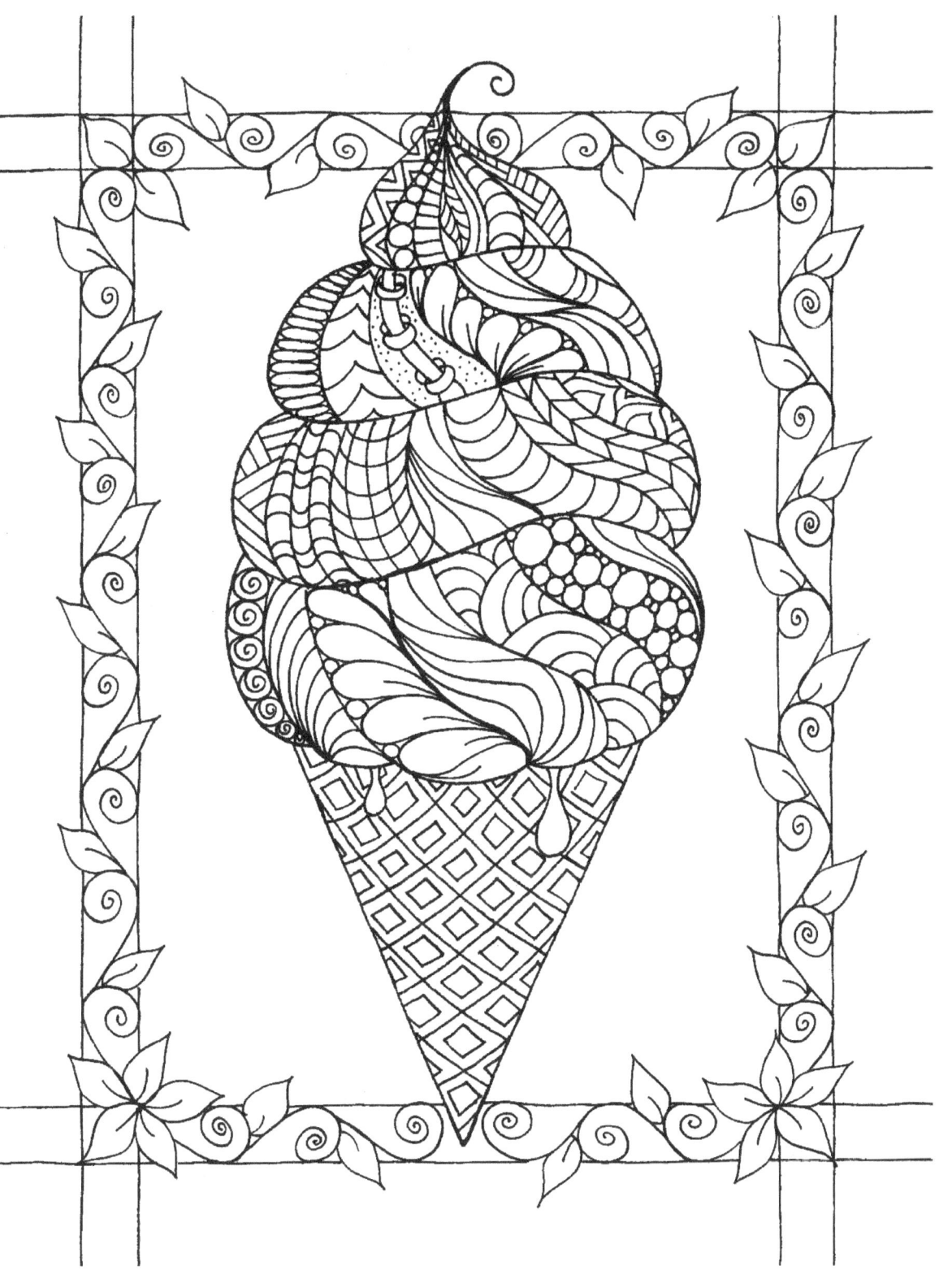

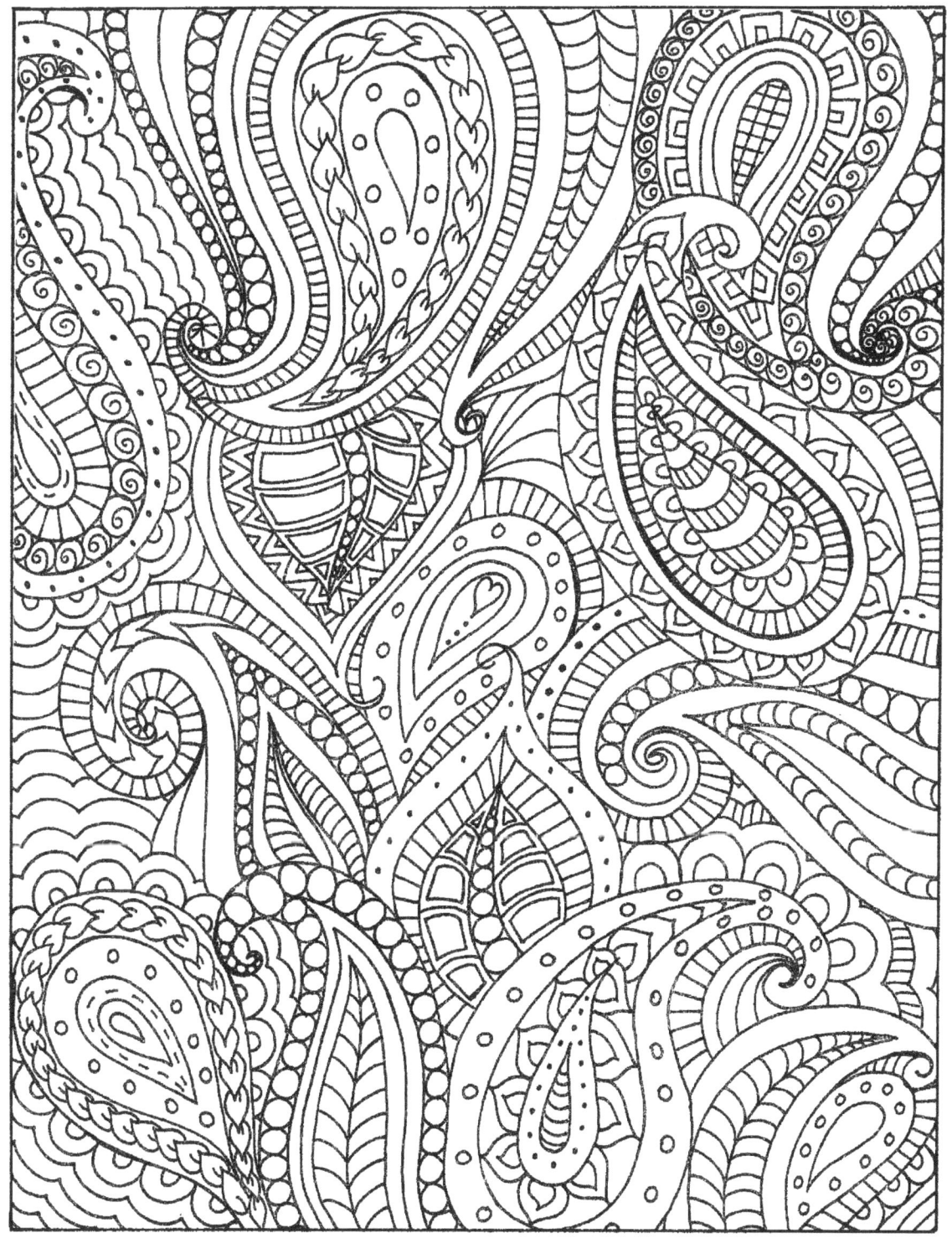

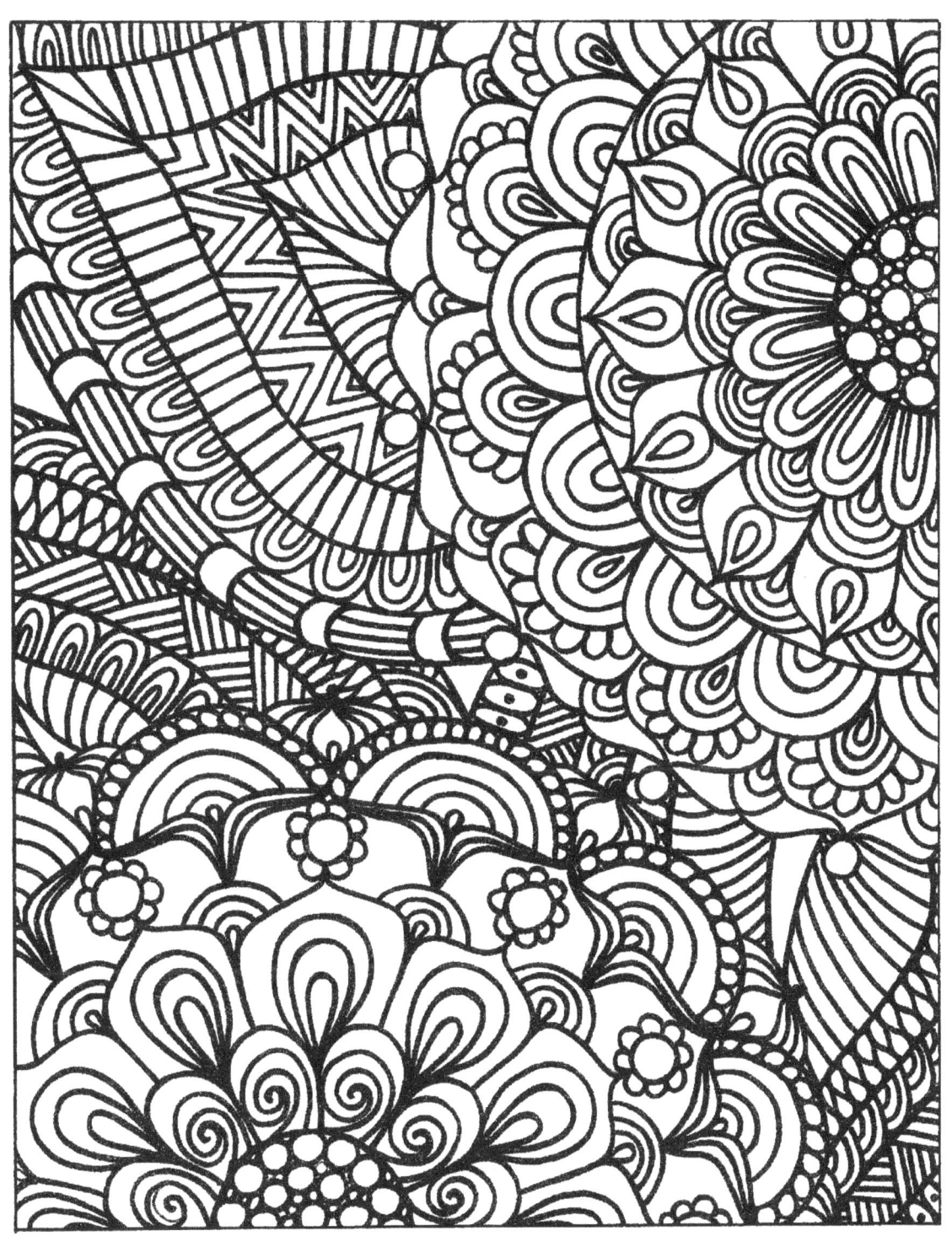

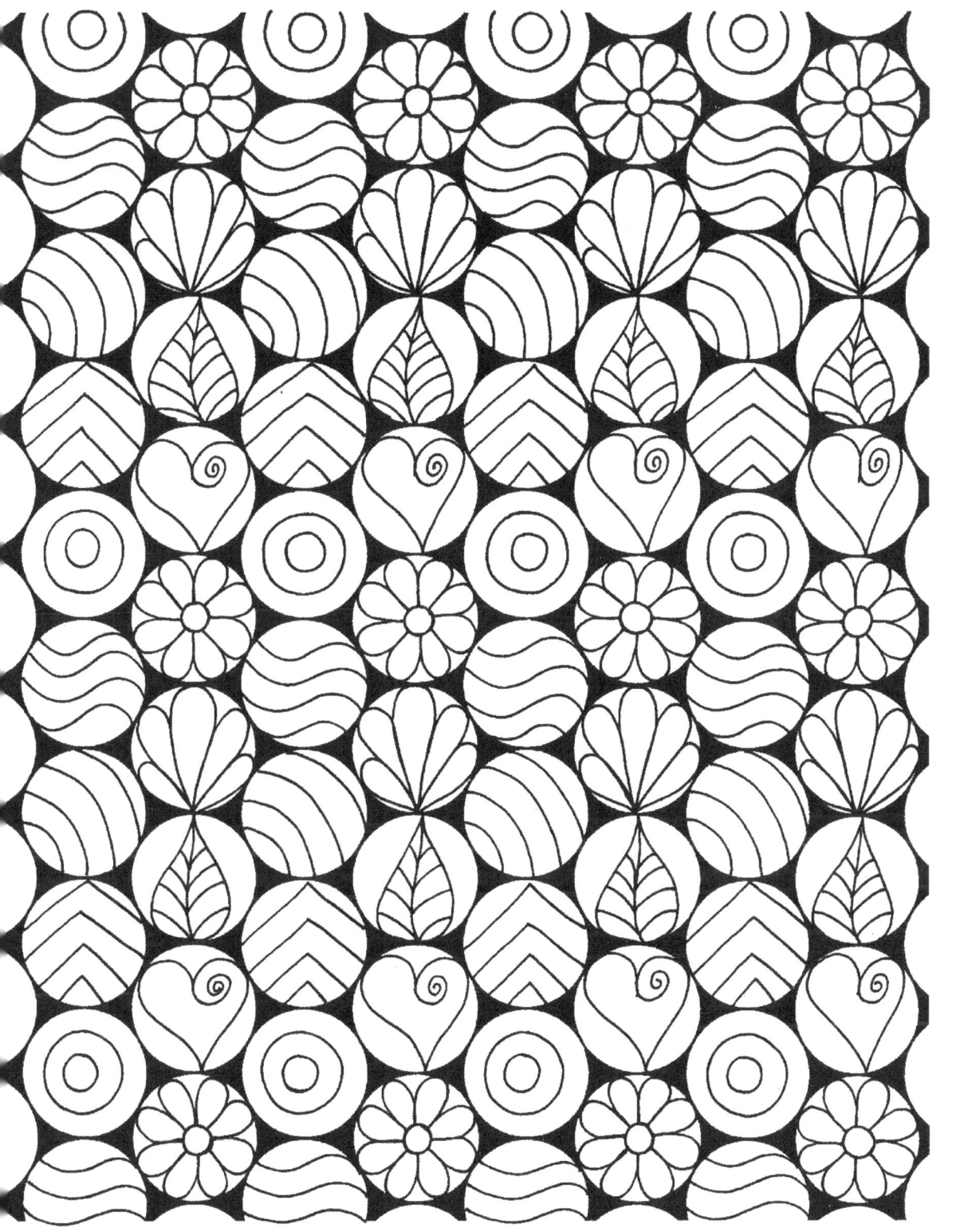

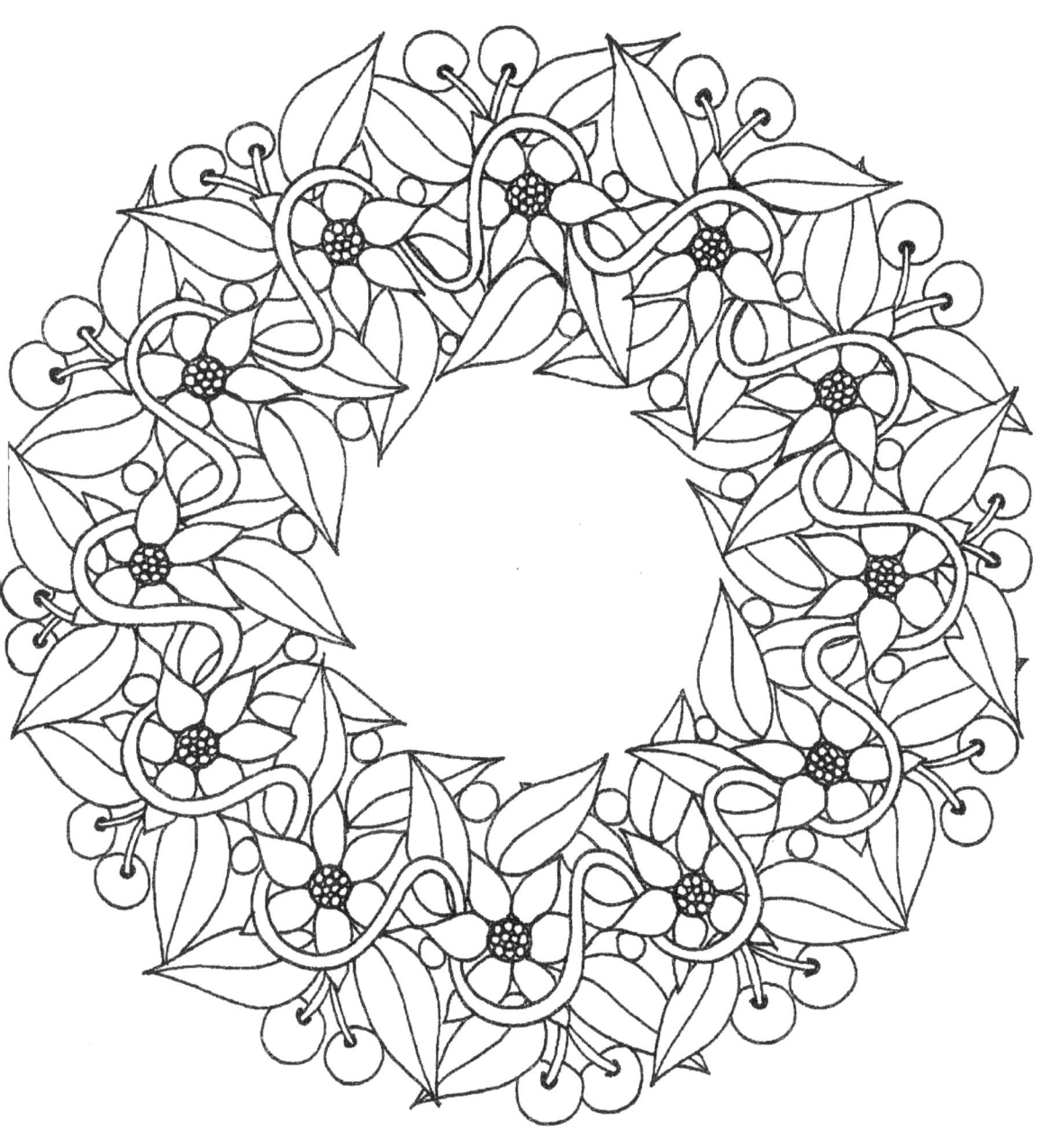

www.ingramcontent.com/pod-product-compliance
Lightning Source LLC
Chambersburg PA
CBHW080538190526
45169CB00007B/2542